Entrepreneurship in Developing Economies: The Bottom Billions and Business Creation

Entrepreneurship in Developing Economies: The Bottom Billions and Business Creation

Paul D. Reynolds

George Washington University
Washington, D.C.
USA
pauldavidsonreynolds@gmail.com

Boston – Delft

Foundations and Trends® in Entrepreneurship

Published, sold and distributed by:
now Publishers Inc.
PO Box 1024
Hanover, MA 02339
USA
Tel. +1-781-985-4510
www.nowpublishers.com
sales@nowpublishers.com

Outside North America:
now Publishers Inc.
PO Box 179
2600 AD Delft
The Netherlands
Tel. +31-6-51115274

The preferred citation for this publication is P. D. Reynolds, Entrepreneurship in Developing Economies: The Bottom Billions and Business Creation, Foundations and Trends® in Entrepreneurship, vol 8, no 3, pp 141–277, 2012.

ISBN: 978-1-60198-953-6
© 2012 P. D. Reynolds

Foundations and Trends® in Entrepreneurship
Volume 8 Issue 3, 2012
Editorial Board

Editorial Scope

Foundations and Trends® in Entrepreneurship will publish survey and tutorial articles in the following topics:

- Nascent and start-up entrepreneurs
- Opportunity recognition
- New venture creation process
- Business formation
- Firm ownership
- Market value and firm growth
- Franchising
- Managerial characteristics and behavior of entrepreneurs
- Strategic alliances and networks
- Government programs and public policy
- Gender and ethnicity

- New business financing
  - Business angels
  - Bank financing, debt, and trade credit
  - Venture capital and private equity capital
  - Public equity and IPO's
- Family-owned firms
- Management structure, governance and performance
- Corporate entrepreneurship
- High technology
  - Technology-based new firms
  - High-tech clusters
- Small business and economic growth

Information for Librarians

Foundations and Trends® in Entrepreneurship, 2012, Volume 8, 6 issues. ISSN paper version 1551-3114. ISSN online version 1551-3122. Also available as a combined paper and online subscription.

Foundations and Trends® in
Entrepreneurship
Vol. 8, No. 3 (2012) 141–277
© 2012 P. D. Reynolds
DOI: 10.1561/0300000045

Entrepreneurship in Developing Economies: The Bottom Billions and Business Creation[*]

Paul D. Reynolds

Research Professor of Management, School of Business, George Washington University, Washington, D.C., USA, pauldavidsonreynolds@gmail.com

Abstract

Over 100 million of the 1.8 billion midlife adults living on less than $15 a day are attempting to create new firms. Another 110 million are managing new ventures. This is almost half of the global total of 450 million individuals involved with 350 million start-ups and new ventures. They are responsible for almost half of all new firms and one-third of new firm jobs. For the poor, business creation provides more social and personal benefits than illegal and dangerous migration, criminal endeavors, or terrorism. Almost all of the business creation by the bottom billions occurs in developing countries, half are in Asia. The ventures initiated by the bottom billion are a significant proportion of all firms expecting growth, exports, an impact on their markets, and

---

[*] Ayman El Tarabishy suggested using the GEM data set to explore this topic resulting in the first draft of the assessment dated 7 December 2011. This substantial revision reflects suggestion made by Tomasz M. Mcikiewicz to adjust all measures of income to a harmonized global standard, proposals by Erkko Autio to use multi-level modeling to examine the relative impacts of individual and national factors, and comments from Elena Bardasi that more complete information about the basis for developing the estimates of daily income would be helpful. The author alone is, of course, responsible for any errors of omission or commission.

in high tech sectors. Assessments based on multi-level modeling suggest that young adults, whether they are rich or poor, in countries with access to informal financing and an emphasis on traditional, rather than secular-rational, and self-expressive values are more likely to identify business opportunities and feel confident about their capacity to implement a new firm. Such entrepreneurial readiness is, in turn, associated with more business creation. Compared to the strong associations of informal institutions with business creation, formal institutions have very modest and idiosyncratic relationships. Expansion of access to secondary education and early stage financing may be the most effective routes to more firm creation among the bottom billion.

Contents

1

Introduction

The poor also have the right to buy and sell.

(Salem Bouaszizi, brother of Takek Bouazizi, self-immolated in Tunisia after confrontation with government officials, triggering the Arab Spring. uprisings. Hernando de Soto, 2011.)

Of the 7 billion world citizens, about 2 billion are surviving on very little, estimates range from less than \$1.50 to \$4.00 per day.[1] Most of these, more than half, are adults in their economically productive years, from 18 to 64 years old. This challenge has been exacerbated by the global recession, the stagnation that developed after 2007, leading to a shortfall in jobs for both current and future workforces.[2] It is estimated that between 2007 and 2011 the advanced economies have lost 27 million jobs and the developing countries 53 million jobs.[3] Given

---

[1] The lower estimate (\$1.50 per day) is based on summary data provided in Shah, Anup, global Issues "http://www.global issues.org," updated September 20, 2010; the higher estimate (\$4.00 per day) is for 2006 from Pinkovskiy and Sala-i-Martin (2009, Table 2.2).
[2] ILO (2010, 2011).
[3] ILO (2011, pp. vii–viii).

1

the higher birth rates in developing countries, the total "job shortfall" can be expected to increase in the next several decades. Providing these individuals with a way to contribute to the global economy is a major challenge.[4] This clearly has major consequences for the bottom billions.

Several strategies for including the bottom billion in the world economy have been proposed. The original assessments focused on improvements in national attributes and institutions.[5] Another focus has been to encourage major multi-national corporations to expand their sales and production operations to include "the poor." As the aggregate demand among the bottom billions is substantial, this could be quite profitable.[6] It has also been proposed that providing assistance to high potential new and small firms may provide jobs for this emerging mass of young adults. This reflects substantial research in developed countries that indicate a small percentage of high growth firms are responsible for a substantial proportion of job creation. A number of such initiatives have recently been launched, often associated with a "toolkit" to guide the indigenous business owners.[7]

The focus on high growth firms as a solution to the jobs shortfall has several complications. First, the net impact of efforts to assist several hundred or even several thousand new and small firms is likely to be small, given that tens of millions of jobs need to be created. For example, Egypt alone has about 3.4 million citizens in the start-up (pre-profit) stage of business creation; assisting several hundred new or small Egyptian firms may provide some interesting success stories, but may not have much overall impact.

More significant, all the research on "gazelle" job creation compares these firms to others that were started at the same time; they do not track the basis for the job growth or the effect on the total system. Much of the job growth of the high flyers comes at the expense of their competitors, who may be driven out of business, or from purchases of competing firms. The net job growth in the system may be very small. The dominant firm in job growth in the United States has been

---

[4] Goldstone (2010).
[5] Collier (2007).
[6] Prahalad (2010).
[7] Weidemann Associates (2011).

Wal-Mart, which went from zero employees to 2 million in 50 years. Despite the multiple benefits to the consumer, the net jobs in retail did not increase, they were just redeployed.

The options for the bottom billions are limited. Many would prefer to find stable, well-paying employment. This has led to the proposals that public policy, particularly in advanced countries, should emphasize job creation, rather than appeasement of financial markets.[8] The lack of employment opportunities has been associated with higher rates of social discontent, which may be exacerbated by dramatic levels of income inequality found in developing countries.[9] It has been one of the major factors leading to the Arab Spring uprisings.

But the absence of employment has also led to substantial economic migration, as those in desperate straits make their way to more promising labor markets. This often involves very risky and dangerous travel over circuitous routes across the Pacific, the Mediterranean, the Caribbean, deserts and into jungles.[10] Reports of deaths and abuses by "transportation agents" are, unfortunately, commonplace. Economic desperation is also the major motivation that makes young women susceptible to "employment offers" that lead to forced participation in sex trafficking.[11]

Other options, fortunately chosen by a small minority, involve criminal activity in various forms, such as engaging in piracy off Somalia, participating in kidnapping gangs in Latin America, joining the mafia in Russia, or, in order to make their mark in the world, pursuing terrorism. None of these choices provide positive social benefits and participants generally have a short life span.

But another choice is to pursue business creation. There has been some attention to facilitation of business creation among the bottom billions. The micro-finance programs associated with the Grameen

---

[8] ILO (2011, p. viii).

[9] Milanovic (2005, 2011).

[10] In early 2012, thousands of Haitians have found their way into the upper Amazon of Brazil, seeing construction work (Romero, 2012); apparently being well treated by the local and national authorities.

[11] Milanovic (2011) provides a wealth of examples, from literature and real life, related to life choices — some desperate and risky — in response to various forms of income inequality.

Bank in Bangladesh has been the basis for expansion to other develop-ing countries.[12] The overall impact of these programs, despite individ-ual examples of dramatic success, has been mixed, in part because a substantial portion of the micro-finance support is used to benefit poor households in ways not related to business creation.

Approaches to assist the bottom billions would be more effective if there was a better understanding of the extent to which "the poor" are already involved in business creation and the nature of the ventures they pursue. For example, worldwide over 200 million are in the start-up or pre-profit stage of business creation. If one in three is able to create a profitable job for him or herself,[13] it would cover a substantial proportion of the 80 million employment shortfall mentioned above. The following assessment develops such a description using a unique data source that has only recently become available.

Initiated in 1999, the Global Entrepreneurship Monitor (GEM) pro-gram has involved harmonized surveys of representative samples of the adult populations in 77 countries, many of which are in the developing world.[14] It can be used to determine the nature and extent of business creation by those at all levels of economic status, advantaged and dis-advantaged. The analysis is based on data from 836,958 interviews from 74 countries that have the necessary data. These estimates are provided for eight global regions, encompassing the entire world. While there is certainly a margin of error in all estimates, the major differences are dramatic and provide useful first estimates regarding the prevalence and amount of business creation by those with different levels of daily income.

The assessment has five components. First, there is a review of the procedure used to identify the bottom billions, which is based on estimates of annual income converted to daily income in 2009 US dollars adjusted for purchasing power parity (the procedure is outlined

---

[12] Bornstein (2011).

[13] Longitudinal studies of business creation in the United States have found that after 6 years of effort about one-third of start-up ventures report a period of profitability (Reynolds and Curtin, 2011).

[14] An overview of the research and the procedure for assembling the data set is provided in Appendix A, more details on the program are provided in Reynolds et al. (2005) and on the project Web site, "www.gemconsortium.org."

in Appendix B). For convenience, five groups are identified for analysis, with daily per capita incomes of US$6.32, US$10.25, US$ 20.61, US$ 46.20, and US$ 143.88. Their global distribution and personal characteristics are reviewed.

The second section reviews the relationship of different levels of daily income with participation in two initial stages of the firm life cycle: nascent entrepreneurs in the pre-profit or start-up stage and owner-managers of new firms, those profitable for 3 to 42 months. Among the 1.8 billion midlife adults living on less than $15 a day over 100 million are attempting to create new firms and over 110 million are managing a new venture; most are in developing, low income countries.

The third section considers the personal characteristics of those active in business creation. For example, about two in five are women, and the proportion of women is greater among those with less daily income. The effect of personal characteristics or the tendency to become involved in business creation is also explored.

Because many start-ups are team efforts, the 100 million poor nascent entrepreneurs are working to implement about 52 million nascent ventures; the 110 million poor new firm owners are managing about 80 million new firms. The major features of these ventures and firms — type of the business activity, orientation toward job creation, operating in high technology sectors, expecting a market impact, and sales to out of country customers — is reviewed in the fourth section.

The fifth section identifies the national features and individual characteristics systematically associated with participation in business creation. The predictive success of linear additive models based on multiple regression and multi-level modeling procedures is quite good. Attention to the relative impact of national and individual factors indicates that a personal readiness for entrepreneurship is a critical intervening variable in the firm creation process.

The conclusion provides an overview of the major patterns and explores selected policy implications.

2

Who are the Bottom Billions?

There are several ways to identify individuals based on their economic status. Estimates of daily per capita income have been popular, as they provide a straightforward measure of the relative economic situation that is easy to comprehend. Much attention is given to those at the very lowest levels, those below \$1.50, \$2 or \$4 per day.[1] Regardless of the monetary criterion, it is clear that several billion persons at the bottom of the income distribution are in difficult situations. For this assessment, a procedure was developed to identify those at the bottom of the income distribution.

The daily income in 2009 US dollars, adjusted for purchasing power parity, for the GEM sample, weighted to represent the global population of those 18–64 years of age, is provided in Table 2.1.[2] These five categories were developed from consideration of the distribution across the sample weighted to represent the global population of those 18–64 years old.[3] These estimates are developed from the 836,956 GEM interviews

---

[1] See footnote 1, Section 1, for the sources.

[2] The procedure for developing these financial estimates is described in Appendix B.

[3] The focus on individuals provides strong justification for adjusting the data to represent people, rather than countries. Milanovic (2005) provides multiple examples of the impact of alternative weighting schemes on measure of income and income inequality.

Table 2.1. Mid-career adult population distribution based on daily income.

	Average daily income ($)	Average yearly income ($)	GEM sample ($n = 836,956$) (%)	Global counts (Millions)
$60–$407/day	143.88	52,517	19.5	830
$30–$60/day	46.20	16,865	17.3	733
$15–$30/day	20.61	7,522	19.6	832
$7.50–$15/day	10.25	3,741	17.3	737
$1–$7.50/day	6.32	2,305	26.3	1,116
All categories/total	44.82	16,358	100.0	4,248

completed from 2000 to 2009 from 74 countries where information is available on income for those 18–64 years of age. It is, at this time, the only available data that also includes measures of participation in business creation.

The top two categories, above the US$ 30 per day level, which is about US$ 17,000 per year, represent 1.7 billion or 37% of all those 18–64 years old. The focus of this assessment, however, are the 44% or 1.8 billion individuals[4] reporting daily income of less than $15.00 per day, less than about $5,000 per year. While this level of income is somewhat higher than other estimates of the economic status of the bottom billions, it includes only midlife adults, those between 18 and over 64 years of age. As children and the aged may be associated with lower levels of income, their inclusion would probably reduce the average levels. A substantial proportion of the world population in very disadvantaged economic situations is identified by this procedure.

2.1 Global Distribution by Daily Income

The global distribution of midlife adults, those 18–64 years of age, is presented in Figure 2.1. The estimated count, in thousands, is provided in Table 2.2.[5] The ranking of the regions is designed to optimize

---

[4] These counts are developed by estimating the prevalence for each of eight world regions, described below, multiplied by the number of persons 18–64 years of age in each region.

[5] The classification of regions and location of the 74 GEM countries is presented in Appendix C. The labeling of the four non-European Anglo countries (Australia, Canada, New Zealand, and the United States) as "North America, Oceania" is somewhat awkward, but seems to provide an "unbiased" label.. Others have used "Western Offshoots" to refer to the same group of countries (Milanovic, 2011, p. 143).

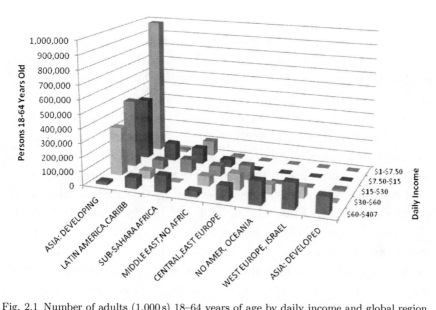

Fig. 2.1 Number of adults (1,000 s) 18–64 years of age by daily income and global region.

Table 2.2. Population counts by daily income and global region (1,000 s).

	Total population	Population 18–64 years old	$60–$407/ day	$30–60/ day	$15–$30/ day	$7.50–$15/ day	$1–$7.50/ day
ASIA: LO INC	3,554,617	2,265,552	19,945	344,400	481,327	438,278	981,602
L AMERICA, CAR	567,671	346,200	79,724	55,691	66,408	128,398	15,980
SUB-SAH AFRICA	797,832	438,596	119,147	—	96,624	115,096	107,728
M EAST,N AFRIC	411,420	248,544	39,759	70,067	74,460	53,529	10,730
CEN,E EUROPE	476,605	322,774	103,260	114,201	103,196	2,117	—
N AMER, OCEANI	370,651	232,513	164,788	67,725	—	—	—
W EUROPE, ISRA	417,773	262,469	182,736	79,733	—	—	—
ASIA: HI INC	211,919	132,271	120,352	1,533	10,386	—	—
Totals	6,808,488	4,248,919	829,710	733,350	832,402	737,418	1,116,040

graphic presentation of the vertical bars, so the regions with the largest populations are presented to the left of Figure 2.1 and the top row of Table 2.2.

The total counts are highest for regions with the most population, Developing Asia, Latin America, and Sub-Sahara Africa. These three regions and the Middle East, North Africa (MENA) region have virtually all (99.9%) of the 1.8 bottom billion in the two lowest daily income categories. This represents over half (56%) of the population in their working years (18–64 years old) in these four regions. In contrast, virtually all (98.3%) of those in the regions with more advanced economies, Developed Asia, Western Europe and Israel, and North American, Oceania, are in the top two categories of daily income.

There are several distinctive features in this presentation of the global distribution. First, the lack of any low income citizens in the high income regions (North America, Oceania; Western Europe, Israel; and Asian Developed) probably reflects the lack of precision in the harmonized measure of annual income. The lack of any responses in Sub-Sahara Africa in the fourth highest category ($30–$60 per day) may reflect both the small number of countries from this region in the GEM sample and the extreme income inequality in this region. Finally, the pattern in Central and Eastern Europe, which is intermediate between the four developing regions and the three advanced regions, which may be consistent with the transition of many of these countries from centralized to market based economies.

2.2   Daily Income and Personal Characteristics[6]

Are those in poor economic situations unique, other than living in low income, developing countries? Information about four demographic characteristics and three orientations as related to level of daily income is presented in Table 2.3.

For example, there are few major differences related to gender.[7] Women compose 52% of those in the lowest income level, but about 47% for the other four highest levels.

---

[6] In this and all following analysis, case weights are assigned to reflect the global distribution of those 18–64 years of age.

[7] Because of the large sample size, over 800,000 cases, virtually all differences — even those in the third decimal place — are highly statistically significant. As a consequence, the discussion will focus on substantive significance.

Table 2.3.　Personal characteristics associated with daily income.

	$60–$407/ day	$30–$60/ day	$15–$30/ day	$7.50–$15/ day	$1–$7.50/ day	All
Gender						
Men	53.3%	54.1%	53.0%	53.1%	48.5%	52.1%
Women	46.7%	45.9%	47.0%	46.9%	51.5%	47.9%
	100.0%	100.0%	100.0%	100.0%	100.0%	100.0%
Age						
18–24 yrs	14.5%	18.9%	19.8%	20.6%	18.0%	18.2%
25–34 yrs	24.8%	27.9%	25.2%	27.9%	25.1%	26.1%
35–44 yrs	25.3%	24.2%	24.7%	23.6%	24.6%	24.5%
45–54 yrs	21.3%	17.2%	18.5%	17.8%	18.8%	18.8%
55–64 yrs	14.0%	11.8%	11.8%	10.2%	13.5%	12.4%
	99.9%	100.0%	100.0%	100.1%	100.0%	100.0%
Education						
No HS degree	16.8%	29.4%	42.9%	60.5%	71.5%	45.2%
HS degree	34.2%	33.3%	29.3%	21.4%	17.2%	26.7%
Post HS	33.0%	24.5%	18.4%	13.9%	7.9%	19.1%
Graduate	15.9%	12.8%	9.4%	4.1%	3.5%	9.0%
	99.9%	100.0%	100.0%	99.9%	100.1%	100.0%
Labor Force Status						
Working	73.7%	71.2%	67.0%	60.6%	63.8%	67.3%
Not working	16.9%	16.6%	20.0%	32.7%	26.6%	22.4%
Not in labor force	9.4%	12.2%	13.0%	6.7%	9.6%	10.3%
	100.0%	100.0%	100.0%	100.0%	100.0%	100.0%
Perspectives						
Readiness for entrepreneurship	1.88	1.98	1.97	1.97	1.86	1.93
See opportunity	30.7%	30.9%	33.4%	40.5%	32.2%	33.3%
Know entrepreneur	43.7%	54.7%	54.0%	42.6%	45.3%	48.0%
Have skills	50.0%	50.1%	47.0%	58.2%	40.5%	48.1%
Fear of failure	31.3%	30.0%	30.9%	33.8%	29.9%	31.0%
Entrepreneurial climate	2.26	2.41	2.46	2.41	2.45	2.40
Entre good career	59.1%	66.0%	67.0%	64.6%	63.8%	64.3%
Entre hi status	65.0%	69.3%	67.7%	66.6%	67.8%	67.4%
Good media cover	59.0%	69.6%	74.8%	67.4%	70.8%	68.8%

There are more differences related to age. There are a lower proportion of those under 24 years of age in the highest daily income category; about 35% are over 44 years of age in this group. The age distributions for the three middle income categories are very similar. The lowest income category has fewer adults under 24 and more adults over 54 than the three higher categories. There are no major age and gender differences associated with the various levels of daily income in this global assessment. It is possible, however, that when different countries or global regions are considered, age and gender differences may be present.

There are major differences associated with educational attainment, as shown in the third set of rows in Table 2.3. Almost half (49%) of those in the highest daily income category have post high school (secondary school) training, college degrees, or graduate program experience, compared to less than one in eight (12%) of those in the lowest daily income category. Over seven in ten in the lowest daily income category have not completed high school, compared to less than one in six (17%) for the highest daily income group. There is no question of a strong relationship between the level of education and daily income, with the biggest differences across the second ($7.50–$15 per day), third ($15–$30 per day), and fourth ($30–$60 per day) categories, where the proportion without high school degrees is reduced by half, from 60% to 29% and the proportion with post high school experiences doubled, from 18% to 37%.

Participation in the labor force, shown in the fourth block of Table 2.3, reflects a consistent, gradual increase in the proportion of respondents in each income category that are working, from 64% in the lowest category to 74% in the highest category. Again, the biggest difference is between the second and third lowest daily income groups. That being said, the majority in the lowest daily income categories are working. This would suggest they are making an effort to support themselves, but with very mixed success.

Three sets of questions provide information on the respondents' orientation toward business creation. One of the best predictors of participation in business creation is a three item measure of "readiness for entrepreneurship." It is based on yes or no responses to three statements[8]:

- There are good opportunities for starting a business where you live

---

[8] This index has a Chronback's Alpha reliability of 0.50, which is lower than desired but provides a useful measure of an important aspect. The creation of the index is discussed in more detail in Reynolds (2011, p. 94).

- You personally know someone that started a business in the past 2 years
- You have the knowledge, skill, and experience to start a business

Both the index and the proportion providing positive responses to each item are provided in Table 2.3.

The readiness for entrepreneurship index values are lowest for those at the bottom and top of the daily income distribution, and somewhat higher for those in the three intermediate categories. This would suggest that the prevalence of business creation would be higher for these intermediate categories, which is indeed the case (presented below in Table 3.1). But the low and high income groups are low for different reasons. The low income groups are quite low on the confidence they have the skills and knowledge to start a business, the high income groups (representing those living in Western Europe and high income Asian countries) appear to have less contact with entrepreneurs and are less likely to see good business opportunities. They may also be more critical of what constitutes a "good business opportunity."

Responses to a question about the consequences of a fear of failure, "Fear of failure would prevent you from starting a business," are unrelated to the other items in this index.[9] Indeed, it is almost constant across all the income groups, a slightly higher proportion (34%) in the second to the bottom income category say "yes" to this item compared to the overall average (31%).

Perception of a supportive entrepreneurial climate was measured with an index reflecting yes or no responses to three statements:

- In your country, most consider starting a new business a desirable career choice
- In your country, those successful at starting a business have a high level of status and respect
- In your country, you often see stories in the public media about successful new businesses

---

[9] This does not, unfortunately, provide information about the respondent's actual "fear of failure."

Again, they can be used to create an index measuring the perceived entrepreneurial climate.[10]

Previous research with similar measures of the entrepreneurial climate has produced a confounding anomaly; the perception of the entrepreneurial climate is the most positive among those with the least involvement in business creation. Those individuals with greater involvement, such as established business owners, tend to have a more negative judgment than those with no business creation experience.[11]

In the comparison across the various daily income groups, the perception of a supportive context for entrepreneurship is lowest for those with the highest levels of daily income, again reflecting those in Western Europe and high income Asian countries. There is little difference among the other four daily income categories. As shown in the patterns for the three separate items, the high income category is less positive about all three items than any of the other income groups; they are less likely to say entrepreneurship is a good career choice, that successful entrepreneurs have respect, or that there is good media coverage of successful new businesses.

Overall, those in the lowest daily income categories, compared to those in the higher daily income categories:

- Have slightly more women
- May have slightly more older individuals
- Have much less education; over 70% have not completed high (secondary) school
- More than 60% report working, which is somewhat less than the higher income groups.
- They are slightly less ready for entrepreneurship that the three intermediate income groups.

---

[10] The reliability measured by Chronback's Alpha for this index is 0.45, again less than preferred, but it serves as a useful summary measure of judgments about the social support for entrepreneurship. Development of the index is discussed in more detail in Reynolds (2011, p. 96).

[11] Reynolds and White (1997).

- Their fear of failure is relatively low.
- Their perception of community support for entrepreneurship is as high as any other income group.

Aside from the low level of education, they are broadly similar to other groups identified on the basis of daily income.

3

How Much Participation in Business Creation Exists?

Two stages of the firm life course are associated with business creation. The first of these is the nascent or pre-profit stage, when an individual or team begins to assemble the resources and develop a plan for implementing a new firm. If these efforts are effective, the initiative may reach the stage of producing initial profits; achieving positive monthly cash flow is a convenient criterion for identifying a firm birth.

In the GEM research procedure, those that report they have recently been engaged in behavior to implement a new firm, expect to own all or part of the firm, and have not reached a level of initial profits, are considered nascent entrepreneurs and these initiatives are considered nascent ventures. Those that report they are actively managing a firm in which they share ownership that has been profitable for up to 42 months are considered new firm owners and these ventures are considered new firms.

In both cases the individuals provide a range of information about themselves and the new venture. As there are some differences in the individuals and ventures in these two stages of the firm life course, it is useful to keep them separate.

3.1   Nascent Entrepreneurs

The pool of nascent entrepreneurs is constantly changing, as people enter the start-up process and, as complications develop, disengage to pursue other options. Globally, at any given time, there are about 211 million involved. The relationship of participation in business creation and the total counts of nascent entrepreneurs related to daily income are presented in Table 3.1.

While the overall prevalence rate is about 5.0 per 100, the pattern is, more or less, an inverted U-shape, with the highest levels associated with those in intermediate levels of daily income. The lowest prevalence rate at 4.1 per 100 is associated with those with the highest levels of daily income; it increases for those with intermediate levels of daily income, to 5.6, 4.7, and 5.6 per 100, and drops slightly to 5.0 per 100 for those with the lowest levels of daily income. The low level of 4.7 per 100 for the intermediate income category ($15–$30 per day) may be related to the strong representation of Central, Eastern European countries in this income category.

The total amount of activity, as presented in the two right columns of Table 3.1, shows that those in the lowest two income categories, which represent 1.8 billion midlife adults, account for 46% of the total activity, 97 million nascent entrepreneurs. Those in the top two income categories, which represent 1.6 billion midlife adults, account for 35% of the total activity, 75 million nascent entrepreneurs.

Table 3.1.   Nascent entrepreneurs by daily income: global estimate.

Daily income	Number of adults, 18–64 years old (millions)	Percent of adults, 18–64 years old (%)	Prevalence [#/100] of nascent entrepreneurs	Number of nascent entrepreneurs, 18–64 years old (millions)	Percent of nascent entre's (%)
$60–$407	830	19.5	4.1	34	16.1
$30–$60	733	17.3	5.6	41	19.4
$15–$30	832	19.6	4.7	39	18.5
$7.50–$15	737	17.4	5.6	41	19.4
$1–$7.50	1,116	26.3	5.0	56	27.0
All incomes	4,248	100.1	5.0	211	100.0

Table 3.2. Prevalence of nascent entrepreneurs (#/100) by daily income and global region.

Global region	$60–$407/ day	$30–60/ day	$15–$30/ day	$7.50–$15/ day	$1–$7.50/ day	All nascents
Asia: Low Inc	4.4	7.2	4.9	5.4	4.6	5.2
Latin America, Caribb	8.8	9.1	6.7	5.8	7.9	7.3
Sub-Sahara Africa	3.6	—	3.7	6.0	8.1	5.4
Middle East, No Afric	5.4	5.6	6.4	5.5	11.8	6.1
Central,East Europe	2.8	1.9	1.7	3.4	—	2.1
No Amer, Oceania	6.0	5.5	—	—	—	5.9
West Europe, Israel	2.4	2.0	—	—	—	2.3
Asia: Hi Inc	2.0	1.0	2.4	—	—	2.0
All Regions	4.1	5.6	4.7	5.6	5.1	5.1

The prevalence rates (#/100 persons 18–64 years of age) are presented by global region and daily income in Table 3.2.[1] The patterns among the prevalence rates show some variation. In only two global regions–North America, Oceania and Western Europe, Israel — is the highest income group associated with the highest prevalence rates of nascent entrepreneurs. But in both regions the difference is small and there are only two income groups. A more detailed assessment of household income for these regions may also reflect a reduced level of activity in the very highest income groups. In all other regions the prevalence rates are greatest in one of the lower income groups. In both Sub-Sahara Africa and the MENA regions the prevalence rates in the lowest income groups is more than twice that of the highest income group.

But the patterns associated with counts of nascent entrepreneurs are quite different, as presented in Figure 3.1 and Table 3.3.

More than half (56% or 118 of 211 billion) of the nascent entrepreneurs are found the developing Asian countries. Over half of this amount (69 million) or 33% of the total is occurring among the two lowest daily income groups in developing Asian countries. Another 30%

---

[1] The nascent prevalence rates by daily income for each GEM country are provided in Appendix D1.

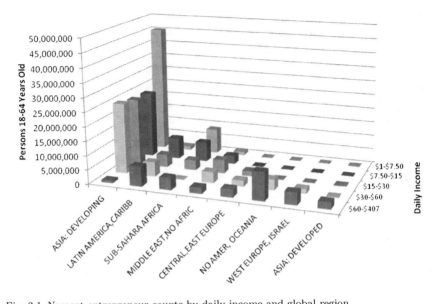

Fig. 3.1 Nascent entrepreneur counts by daily income and global region.

Table 3.3.   Number of nascent entrepreneurs (1,000) by daily income and global region.

Global region	Population: 18–64 Years old	$60–$407/ day	$30–$60/ day	$15–$30/ day	$7.50–$15/ day	$1–$7.50/ day	All
Asia: Low Income	2,265,552	886	24,964	23,730	23,484	45,231	118,296
L. America, Caribb	346,200	7,012	5,064	4,473	7,394	1,260	25,203
Sub-Sahara Africa	438,596	4,255	—	3,538	6,900	8,757	23,450
Mid East, N Afric	248,544	2,161	3,893	4,779	2,962	1,270	15,065
Cent, East Europe	322,774	2,877	2,123	1,773	73	—	6,847
N Amer, Oceania	232,513	9,901	3,720	—	—	—	13,621
W Europe, Israel	262,469	4,318	1,617	—	—	—	5,935
Asia: Hi Inc	132,271	2,410	16	247	—	—	2,673
All Regions	4,248,919	33,820	41,398	38,541	40,813	56,517	211,089

(or 64 million) is occurring in the other three developing regions, Latin
America, MENA, and Sub-Sahara Africa. Eastern and Western Europe
have a combined share of 6% (13 million nascents), about equal to that

of the four North American, Oceania countries (14 million nascents or 6.5%). Activity is by far the lowest among the developed Asian countries, with 2.7 million nascents representing 1.3% of the total.

Given this dramatic variation, associated with income levels and global regions, it is of interest to consider both the character of individuals involved as well as the ventures being pursued. This is discussed following a review of the presence of new firm owners.

3.2 New Firm Owners

The second stage of the business life course is that of a new firm, one that has recently achieved profitability. New firm owners are those individuals indentified as actively involved in the management of a business, that are the sole or part owners, and that have reported profits for 3 to 42 months. Their prevalence rate and numbers by economic status are presented in Table 3.4.

The pattern is somewhat different from that of nascent entrepreneurs. The prevalence rate is lowest, 3.6 per 100, for those with the highest daily income ($60–407 per day). It increases to 6.5 per 100 for those in the next highest level ($30–$60 per day), then drops slightly for those at the lowest level ($1–$7.50 per day) to 6.4 per 100. This would suggest that many with the highest daily incomes have found more lucrative positions in established organizations, are in well paying professions, or, perhaps, have private wealth.

Table 3.4.   New firm owners by daily income: global estimate.

Daily income	Number of adults, 18–64 years old (millions)	Percent of adults, 18–64 years old (%)	Prevalence [#/100] of new firm owners	Number of new firm owners, 18–64 years old (millions)	Percent of new firm owners (%)
$60–$407	830	19.5	3.6	30	12.7
$30–$60	733	17.3	6.5	48	20.4
$15–$30	832	19.6	5.4	45	19.1
$7.50–$15	737	17.4	5.6	41	17.4
$1–$7.50	1,116	26.3	6.4	72	30.2
All incomes	4,178	100.1	5.6	236	100.0

The overall pattern related to daily income is similar to that of nascent entrepreneurs, with the 37% in the two highest daily income categories accounting for 78 million new business owners or 33% of the total. The 45% in the two lowest daily income categories account for 113 million new firm owners or 48% of the total.

The prevalence rates of new firm owners by global region and daily income is presented in Table 3.5.[2] The overall prevalence rates are slightly higher among the developing countries, particularly low income Asia, Latin America and the Caribbean, and Sub-Sahara Africa.

There is considerable diversity among regions in the prevalence rate by daily income. It is very high among those with high daily income in the developing (low national income) Asian region, over four times that among the developed (high national income) Asian region. It is relatively low for the Western Europe, Israel region for both daily income levels. There is a much higher prevalence rate in the two lowest daily income levels than the higher daily income in the Sub-Sahara African region, but this may reflect the small sample in this region.

Table 3.5.   New firm owner prevalence (#/100) by daily income and global region.

	$60–$407/day	$30–$60/day	$15.01–$30.00/day	$7.51–$15.00/day	$1.00–$7.50/day	All
Asia: Low Inc	13.54	11.09	7.11	5.72	5.07	6.62
L. America, Caribb	7.27	3.82	8.16	5.27	10.64	6.30
Sub-Sahara Africa	1.68	—	1.14	6.73	18.72	7.07
Mid East, N Afric	4.08	3.97	3.67	2.43	1.17	3.45
Central, E Europe	3.15	2.03	0.84	1.40	—	2.00
N Amer, Oceania	4.22	2.27	—	—	—	3.65
W Europe, Israel	2.15	1.37	—	—	—	1.91
Asia: Hi Inc	3.30	0.32	4.62	—	—	3.37
All Regions	3.60	6.50	5.40	5.60	6.40	5.55

---

[2] Prevalence rates for new firm owners by country and income level are provided in Table D2.1.

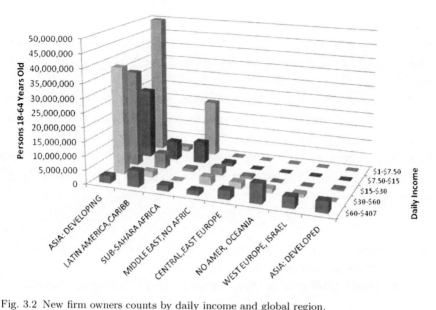

Fig. 3.2 New firm owners counts by daily income and global region.

Table 3.6. New firm owner counts (1000 s) by daily income and global region.

	Population 18–64 years old	$60–$407/day	$30–$60/day	$15.01–$30.00/day	$7.51–$15.00/day	$1.00–$7.50/day	All
Asia: Low Inc	2,265,552	2,700	38,187	34,201	25,053	49,814	149,955
Latin America, Caribb	346,200	5,798	2,130	5,421	6,766	1,700	21,815
Sub-Sah Africa	438,596	1,998	—	1,102	7,750	20,165	31,014
Mid East, N Afric	248,544	1,624	2,784	2,732	1,298	125	8,563
Central, E Europe	322,774	3,252	2,319	863	30	—	6,464
N Amer, Oceania	232,513	6,956	1,539	—	—	—	8,494
W Europe, Israel	262,469	3,921	1,094	—	—	—	5,015
Asia: Hi Inc	132,271	3,968	5	480	—	—	4,453
All Regions	4,248,919	30,217	48,057	44,799	40,896	71,804	235,774

The patterns associated with a total count of new firms owners, as shown in Figure 3.2 and Table 3.6 reflects the number of midlife adults in each region. The patterns found among the nascent entrepreneurs related to global regions are also present regarding new firm owners. For the four "advanced" regions new firm owners are concentrated among the higher daily income groups; for the four developing regions, they have an equal or greater presence among the lower economic status groups.

There are very few new firm owners among the lowest daily income group in five regions, but high counts in three, Sub-Sahara Africa, Latin America, and Developing Asia. These three regions have 203 million new firm owners, or 86% of the total. In fact, almost half, 112 million or 47%, are found in the two lowest income groups in these three developing regions.

Major patterns seem to be that:

- New firm owners are present in all regions and all levels of economic status
- About 90% of new firm owners are in developing regions, 60% in developing Asian countries.
- In developed or high national income regions, more new firm owners are present among those with higher daily incomes.
- In developing, or low national income regions, more new firm owners are present among those with the lowest daily incomes.

4

Who is Involved?

Who is involved in business creation? Are there differences associated with different levels of daily income? Are they different from other midlife adults? There are several ways to explore these issues. One is to describe those involved as nascent entrepreneurs or new firm owners with different levels of daily income. For example, the ages of nascent entrepreneurs with different levels of daily income can be compared. Another is to consider how they differ from typical adults by comparing the tendency of those of different ages to participate in business creation. Both assessments are reviewed after consideration of two important personal features, gender and contextual motivation, are discussed.

4.1 Women

Of the 211 million involved as nascent entrepreneurs about 79 million, or 37%, are women; among the 236 million new firm owners about 100 million, or 42%, are women. The proportion of women by global region and daily income serving as principals of nascent ventures is presented in Table 4.1 and as new firm owners in Table 4.2.

Table 4.1.   Percentage of women among nascent entrepreneurs by daily income and global region.

	$60–$407/ day (%)	$30–$60/ day (%)	$15–$30/ day (%)	$7.50–$15/ day (%)	$1–$7.50/ day (%)	All
Asia: Developing	39	38	35	30	41	37
Latin America, Caribb	38	45	43	49	44	44
Sub-Sahara Africa	45	—	49	37	41	42
Middle East, N Afric	17	22	31	40	33	29
Central, East Europe	28	36	34	28	—	32
N Amer, Oceania	36	43	—	—	—	38
West Europe, Israel	31	35	—	—	—	32
Asia: Developed	36	42	26	—	—	35
All Regions	35	38	36	35	41	37

As can be seen in Table 4.1 there is variation in the involvement of women in nascent ventures. It is slightly higher (41%) in the lowest daily income category than in the other four categories, which range from 35 to 38%. Regional variation is somewhat greater. It is the lowest in the MENA region (29%) and highest in Latin American, Caribbean countries (44%), closely followed by Sub-Sahara Africa (42%). Developing Asian (37%) and North America, Oceania (38%) have slightly less participation. Eastern and Western Europe are equal and somewhat lower (32%) that developed Asian countries (35%).

Similar patterns are found among the proportion of new firm owners that are women related to the global regions, presented in Table 4.2. The proportion is the lowest in the MENA region at 21%, and highest, at 47%, in the Latin American, Caribbean and Sub-Sahara African regions. Women are exactly half (50%) of all new firm owners in the lowest daily income group, and this declines to about one-third (35%) among the highest income groups.

Perhaps the most significant general patterns are:

- Women are a significant number of those involved in all regions and at all income levels. They are 79 million, or 37% of the total, of all nascent entrepreneurs and 100 million, or 42% of the total, of all new firm owner managers.

Table 4.2. Percentage of women among new firm owners by daily income and global region.

	$60–$407/ day (%)	$30–$60/ day (%)	$15–$30/ day (%)	$7.50–$15/ day (%)	$1–$7.50/ day (%)	All
Asia: Developing	49	38	42	34	51	43
Latin America, Caribb	38	47	48	52	52	47
Sub-Sahara Africa	43	—	46	45	48	47
Middle East, N Afric	21	21	19	26	17	21
Central, East Europe	33	44	40	68	—	38
N Amer, Oceania	37	47	—	—	—	39
West Europe, Israel	33	35	—	—	—	34
Asia: Developed	22	28	37	—	—	24
All Regions	35	38	42	39	50	42

- There is no region or daily income group without a substantial proportion of women involved as nascent entrepreneurs or new firm owners, although they are a smaller proportion in the MENA region.
- Women are more involved in business creation in the lower daily income groups.

4.2 Contextual Motivation

All those active in the business life course are asked about their reasons for pursuing new firm creation. They have a choice between reporting they were pursuing a promising business opportunity or reacting to a lack of "good opportunities for work." Both choices can be considered a reaction to the context. About 149 million or 71% of nascent entrepreneurs report they are voluntarily pursuing a business opportunity, referred to as opportunity entrepreneurs; 62 million (29%) report they have no better choices for work, referred to as necessity entrepreneurs. The proportion of nascent entrepreneurs reporting they are motivated by necessity is presented in Table 4.3 by daily income and global region.

There are systematic differences in the proportion of necessity entrepreneurs related to both the global region and level of daily

Table 4.3.   Proportion of necessity nascent entrepreneurs by daily income and global region.

	$60–$407/ day (%)	$30–$60/ day (%)	$15–$30/ day (%)	$7.50–$15/ day (%)	$1–$7.50/ day (%)	All
Asia: Developing	11	28	30	28	38	32
Latin America, Caribb	19	23	32	36	45	28
Sub-Sahara Africa	36	—	33	31	38	35
Middle East, N Africa	27	21	18	17	42	22
Central, East Europe	18	29	39	44	—	27
N Amer, Oceania	11	23	—	—	—	14
West Europe, Israel	15	28	—	—	—	18
Asia: Developed	20	39	34	—	—	22
All Regions	18	26	30	29	39	29

income. The proportion reporting necessity based motivation is higher for those from lower daily income categories and developing countries, reaching 45% in the lowest income groups in the Latin America, Caribbean region. It is lowest for those from high daily income groups in the developed regions, at 11% for North American, Oceania high income nascents and 11% for those from the Western Europe, Israel region.

Among new firm owners, presented in Table 4.4, the proportion that claim they could find "no better choices for work" is systematically higher, the overall ratio is 49% compared to 29% for the nascent entrepreneurs. The overall patterns are the same, with the highest proportions among those from lower daily income categories and developing countries. Once again, the proportion is lowest among high daily income categories in North America, Oceania (13%) and Western Europe, Israel countries (19%). It is the highest in the lowest income categories in the developing Asian (70%) and Central, Eastern European (80%) regions.

One of the more dramatic patterns is that for every global region and daily income level, the proportion that report they have "no better choices for work" is higher among the new firm owners. This would suggest that nascent entrepreneurs, if they have managed to develop a profitable new firm find it more rewarding than other work choices. For

Table 4.4.   Proportion of necessity new firm owners by daily income and global region.

	$60–$407/ day (%)	$30–$60/ day (%)	$15–$30/ day (%)	$7.50–$15/ day (%)	$1–$7.50/ day (%)	All
Asia: Developing	26	40	51	43	70	53
Latin America, Caribb	30	44	46	61	64	48
Sub-Sahara Africa	46	—	48	41	58	53
Middle East, N Afric	40	29	34	44	38	35
Central, East Europe	24	38	54	80	—	33
N Amer, Oceania	13	32	—	—	—	16
West Europe, Israel	19	34	—	—	—	22
Asia: Developed	37	49	74	—	—	42
All Regions	26	39	50	46	66	49

new firm owners, business creation — which may have been a response to undesirable work options — has led to a career that is more desirable than current work-for-pay options. This is particularly true among those in the lowest daily income levels in developing countries.

This suggests that many of those with the skill, resources, or luck to complete the transition from a nascent venture to a profitable new firm find the rewards quite satisfying.

4.3   Characteristics of Participants in Business Creation

The focus of this assessment is on the nature of those with limited resources that are engaged in business creation. A comparison of those actively involved as nascent entrepreneurs with different levels of daily income is presented in Table 4.5, a similar comparison of new firm owners is provided in Table 4.6.

The overall proportion of women is about the same for both stages of firm creation, albeit slightly higher (42%) among new firm owners compared to nascent entrepreneurs (38%). In both stages of firm creation women have a greater representation among those with lower daily income. Women are about one-third of both nascent entrepreneurs and new firm owners in the highest daily income group, but they are

Table 4.5.   Personal characteristics of nascent entrepreneurs by daily income.

	$60–$407/ day	$30–$60/ day	$15–$30/ day	$7.50–$15/ day	$1–$7.50/ day	All
Gender						
Men	66.4%	61.5%	62.1%	62.9%	59.6%	62.2%
Women	33.6%	38.5%	37.9%	37.1%	40.4%	37.8%
	100.0%	100.0%	100.0%	100.0%	100.0%	100.0%
Age						
18–24 yrs	16.8%	21.7%	27.7%	25.0%	26.6%	23.7%
25–34 yrs	32.5%	38.9%	30.3%	33.2%	30.7%	33.2%
35–44 yrs	26.4%	23.2%	22.1%	24.8%	23.8%	24.0%
45–54 yrs	17.5%	11.5%	14.3%	12.5%	12.5%	13.5%
55–64 yrs	6.7%	4.7%	5.5%	4.5%	6.4%	5.6%
	99.9%	100.0%	99.9%	100.0%	100.0%	100.0%
Education						
No HS Degree	13.2%	20.3%	33.4%	46.6%	56.7%	35.1%
HS degree	29.9%	32.3%	30.1%	25.9%	27.1%	29.1%
Post HS	39.1%	32.1%	25.1%	20.5%	10.8%	24.7%
Graduate	17.8%	15.3%	11.5%	7.0%	5.4%	11.1%
	100.0%	100.0%	100.1%	100.0%	100.0%	100.0%
Working Status						
Working	79.8%	84.4%	78.4%	74.2%	76.0%	78.7%
Not working	14.4%	10.7%	14.6%	20.8%	18.0%	15.6%
Not in labor force	5.8%	4.9%	7.0%	5.1%	6.0%	5.7%
	100.0%	100.0%	100.0%	100.1%	100.0%	100.0%
Relative HH Inc						
Upper third	68.1%	68.5%	25.0%	0.9%	0.0%	31.9%
Middle third	30.0%	16.1%	64.7%	66.5%	3.6%	32.6%
Lowest third	1.9%	15.4%	10.3%	32.6%	96.4%	35.5%
	100.0%	100.0%	100.0%	100.0%	100.0%	100.0%
Perspectives						
Entrep Readiness	2.48	2.45	2.43	2.48	2.27	2.41
See opportunity	59.4%	53.2%	56.9%	67.5%	56.6%	58.1%
Know entrepreneur	71.7%	77.7%	76.0%	65.6%	62.7%	70.6%
Have skills	86.9%	76.8%	76.1%	86.3%	66.3%	77.2%
Fear of failure:Yes	22.5%	25.5%	30.4%	28.1%	29.5%	27.3%
Entrep Climate	2.40	2.55	2.57	2.50	2.57	2.53
Entre good career	67.8%	73.7%	77.0%	69.7%	72.1%	72.4%
Entre hi status	71.6%	74.1%	68.5%	68.5%	72.2%	71.3%
Good media cover	67.0%	78.4%	82.4%	74.9%	78.3%	76.9%

40% of nascent entrepreneurs and 52% of new firm owners in the lowest daily income group.

Early midlife adults, 25–44 years in age, are highly represented at both stages of business creation; overall they are 57% of nascent entrepreneurs and 62% of new firm owners. Among the lowest income

Table 4.6.   Personal characteristics of new firm owners by daily income.

	$60–$407/ day	$30–$60/ day	$15–$30/ day	$7.50–$15/ day	$1–$7.50/ day	All
Gender						
Men	65.0%	61.6%	56.8%	59.6%	48.5%	57.5%
Women	35.0%	38.4%	43.2%	40.4%	51.5%	42.5%
	100.0%	100.0%	100.0%	100.0%	100.0%	100.0%
Age						
18–24 yrs	13.3%	18.9%	20.1%	18.6%	11.0%	16.5%
25–34 yrs	33.2%	37.6%	36.1%	39.9%	33.2%	36.0%
35–44 yrs	28.2%	24.7%	25.9%	21.6%	26.9%	25.5%
45–54 yrs	17.3%	13.0%	13.2%	13.2%	20.1%	15.4%
55–64 yrs	7.9%	5.8%	4.7%	6.7%	8.7%	6.7%
	99.9%	100.0%	100.0%	100.0%	99.9%	100.1%
Education						
No HS Degree	17.2%	34.8%	50.6%	59.6%	76.6%	50.2%
HS degree	29.6%	32.6%	27.4%	22.4%	15.6%	25.2%
Post HS	35.3%	19.3%	15.1%	15.1%	6.0%	16.6%
Graduate	17.8%	13.4%	6.9%	2.9%	1.8%	8.0%
	99.9%	100.0%	100.0%	100.0%	100.0%	100.0%
Working Status						
Working	94.0%	96.7%	93.6%	90.6%	94.7%	94.1%
Not working	4.4%	2.0%	5.1%	8.1%	4.8%	4.7%
Not in labor force	1.7%	1.4%	1.2%	1.3%	0.5%	1.2%
	100.1%	100.1%	99.9%	100.0%	100.0%	100.0%
Relative HH Inc						
Upper third	73.8%	84.7%	21.6%	1.2%	0.0%	34.7%
Middle third	24.4%	9.1%	73.2%	68.7%	0.3%	33.4%
Lowest third	1.8%	6.3%	5.2%	30.1%	99.7%	31.9%
	100.0%	100.1%	100.0%	100.0%	100.0%	100.0%
Perspectives						
Entrep Readiness	2.35	2.38	2.26	2.29	2.10	2.27
See opportunity	47.7%	44.0%	42.4%	50.2%	41.0%	44.5%
Know entrepreneur	68.2%	77.4%	69.6%	59.8%	56.4%	66.4%
Have skills	83.0%	75.2%	68.5%	78.6%	61.3%	71.9%
Fear of failure:Yes	22.6%	21.5%	27.7%	32.9%	26.0%	26.0%
Entrep Climate	2.44	2.55	2.55	2.53	2.57	2.54
Entre good career	69.9%	72.2%	70.0%	76.2%	74.1%	72.5%
Entre hi status	72.7%	70.4%	71.8%	69.8%	74.4%	71.8%
Good media cover	70.0%	84.6%	82.9%	76.5%	77.6%	79.6%

group, there are slightly more young adults (18–24 years old) among the nascent entrepreneurs, perhaps because those of the same age (18–24 years old) in the highest income groups are involved in education. The age distribution among new firm owners appears slightly older for all daily income levels, although those over 54 years of age are a small minority of nascent entrepreneurs and new firm owners at all income levels.

There are dramatic differences associated with the level of educational attainment at both stages of firm creation. Educational attainment is higher among those with higher levels of daily income. Among nascent entrepreneurs in the lowest income group, 57% have not completed high school, compared to 13% among the highest income group. Among new firm owners, 75% of those in the lowest income group have not completed high school, compared to 17% among the highest income group. Differences related to post high school experiences are just as dramatic. For example, 16% of the lowest daily income nascents report more than a high school degree, compared to 58% of highest daily income nascents. Among new firm owners, the differences are greater, as 8% of the lowest daily income new firm owners report more than a high school degree, compared to 53% of those from the highest daily income group.

Differences in reports of working status by nascent entrepreneurs show less variation across income groups; overall 78% report working full or part time. Another 16% are not working but, presumably, seeking work. Only a small proportion, 6%, would not be considered in the labor force. Virtually all new firm owners at all income levels report they are part of the labor force, over 90% are working, but this may include their roles as a new firm manager.

While the reports of household income were used to classify individuals using harmonized global measures, they can also be used to identify the individual's household income in relation to the country in which they live. Dramatic differences related to the level of daily income are found for both nascent entrepreneurs and new firms owners. In both stages of business creation, those from lower daily income groups are in the lowest relative household income categories; 97% for nascent entrepreneurs and 99% for new firm owners; none are in the highest third of relative household income.

In contrast, the majority of those in the two highest daily income groups are in the upper third of their countries household income distribution, 68% for nascent entrepreneurs and 85% and 74% for new firm owners. This may reflect the modest background and options of those in the low income groups or better work options of those in the high income groups. Those in higher income households with a good education may find suitable work options if their new firms are not doing well, reducing their prevalence. It may well be a combination of both. In any case, there is no question that the relative standing in the business creation process is quite different for those in different daily income groups.

A comparison of three types of personal perspectives is presented. Readiness for entrepreneurship, and the three questions used to create the index, shows a similar pattern for those in both stages of the firm creation process. Those in the lowest income category at both stages of the firm creation process appear less "ready for entrepreneurship" than those in the four higher categories. They are less likely to see opportunities, know an entrepreneur, and consider they have the skill to implement a new firm.

Estimates of the impact of fear of failure, as a factor causing a reluctance to pursue a new firm, is slightly higher among those from the lowest income category, but the overall differences are slight.

Judgments that their country is supportive of business creation show very little variation across daily income categories, although those in the highest income category seem to have the least positive judgments in both the nascent entrepreneur and new firm owner comparisons.

Overall, then, those in the lowest income categories at both stages of business creation are:

- Well represented by women, who are 40% of nascent entrepreneurs and half of new firm owners.
- Represented by slightly more young adults.
- Represented by many with very limited education.
- Working for pay as they engage in business creation.
- Reporting lower relative household incomes than others in their country.
- Lower on measures of readiness for entrepreneurship.
- Not reporting a higher fear of failure.
- Consider their national context positive for business creation.

Those from low income groups are similar to higher income groups in many respects, but distinctive in that more women are involved, they have less education, lower relative household incomes, somewhat less prepared for entrepreneurship, and, as discussed in the previous section, are more likely to be involved because of a lack of other work options.

4.4   Personal Characteristics and Participation in Business Creation

How do these personal attributes affect involvement in business creation? The previous assessment focused on differences among those already involved. It is possible to compare those active in business creation with those that are not involved. This is done for the same set of attributes by computing the effect of different attributes on the prevalence rate, the number per 100 identified as nascent entrepreneurs in Table 4.7 and new firm owners in Table 4.8. The effects of different factors can be considered in relation to the overall rates of participation by daily income, presented in the top row of Tables 4.7 and 4.8.

For example, among those in the lowest daily income group, 4.8 per 100 are considered nascent entrepreneurs and 5.3 per 100 new firm owners, presented in the top row of Tables 4.7 and 4.8. Table 4.7 indicates that among men in the low daily income group, 5.9 per 100 are considered nascent entrepreneurs, compared to 4.8 per 100 women. A small difference related to gender. Table 4.8, however, indicates that the prevalence rates for men and women as firm owners are identical among the lowest daily income group, it is 5.3 per 100 for both.

The association of age and participation are subtle, but there is a clear difference related to the daily income level. Younger adults, 18–24 years of age, have the highest prevalence as nascent entrepreneurs among the lower daily income groups in Table 4.7. It is, however, the next age category, 25–34 years old, that is most active among the two highest income groups. The highest prevalence rates for new firm owners in Table 4.8 are found in this same group, 25–34 years of age, among all daily income groups.

The association of educational attainment and participation as nascent entrepreneurs, shown in Table 4.7, is relatively consistent across

Table 4.7. Prevalence of nascent entrepreneurs (#/100) by personal characteristics and daily income.

	$60–$407/ day	$30–$60/ day	$15–$30/ day	$7.50–$15/ day	$1–$7.50/ day	All
Base prevalence	4.3	5.8	5.4	4.6	4.8	4.9
Gender						
Men	5.3	6.5	6.3	5.4	5.9	5.9
Women	3.1	4.8	4.2	3.7	4.8	3.9
Age						
18–24 yrs	5.0	6.6	6.5	6.5	7.1	6.4
25–34 yrs	5.6	8.0	5.6	6.4	5.9	6.3
35–44 yrs	4.5	5.5	4.2	5.6	4.7	4.8
45–54 yrs	3.5	3.9	3.6	3.8	3.2	3.5
55–64 yrs	2.1	2.3	2.2	2.4	2.3	2.2
Education						
No HS degree	3.4	4.0	3.6	4.1	3.8	3.8
HS degree	3.7	5.6	4.8	6.5	7.6	5.4
Post HS	5.1	7.5	6.3	7.9	6.6	6.4
Graduate	4.8	6.9	5.7	9.0	5.4	6.1
Lab Force Status						
Working	4.7	6.9	5.4	6.5	5.7	5.8
Not working	3.7	3.8	3.4	3.4	3.2	3.4
Not in labor force	2.7	2.3	2.5	4.0	3.0	2.8
Relative HH Inc						
Upper third	5.0	7.4	5.7	11.7		6.1
Middle third	3.7	4.1	4.8	5.4	24.6	4.8
Lowest third	1.4	3.6	2.7	5.3	4.7	4.4
Perspectives						
See opportunity	10.4	12.0	9.4	9.7	9.7	10.2
Know entrepreneur	8.7	9.8	7.7	9.0	7.6	8.5
Have skills	9.2	10.6	9.0	9.5	9.2	9.5
Entre ready: 0	0.6	1.2	1.2	1.0	2.0	1.3
Entre ready: 1	3.0	4.2	3.0	3.0	4.3	3.6
Entre ready: 2	8.4	10.4	8.2	9.5	7.4	8.8
Entre ready: 3	14.7	14.9	13.2	12.8	13.8	13.9
Fear of failure:Yes	3.8	5.9	5.4	4.8	5.5	5.1
Fear of failure:No	6.2	7.6	5.5	6.7	5.9	6.4
Entre good career	6.8	8.6	7.2	7.0	6.9	7.3
Entre hi status	6.5	8.1	6.4	6.7	6.5	6.6
Good media cover	6.6	8.5	6.9	7.5	6.7	7.3
Entre climate: 0	2.8	4.1	2.8	4.0	2.3	3.1
Entre climate: 1	5.4	6.3	5.9	6.2	4.9	5.7
Entre climate: 2	6.2	7.2	5.3	6.5	6.8	6.4
Entre climate: 3	7.4	9.3	7.8	7.4	6.8	7.8

Table 4.8.   Prevalence of new firm owners (#/100) by personal characteristics and daily income.

	$60–$407/ day	$30–$60/ day	$15–$30/ day	$7.50–$15/ day	$1–$7.50/ day	All
Base prevalence	3.9	6.8	6.7	6.0	5.3	5.7
Gender						
Men	4.7	7.8	7.2	6.8	5.3	6.3
Women	2.9	5.7	6.2	5.2	5.3	5.0
Age						
18–24 yrs	3.5	6.8	6.8	5.4	3.2	5.1
25–34 yrs	5.2	9.2	9.7	8.6	7.0	7.9
35–44 yrs	4.3	7.0	7.1	5.5	5.8	5.9
45–54 yrs	3.1	5.1	4.8	4.5	5.7	4.7
55–64 yrs	2.2	3.4	2.7	3.9	3.4	3.1
Education						
No HS degree	4.0	8.0	7.9	5.9	5.7	6.3
HS degree	3.3	6.7	6.3	6.3	4.8	5.4
Post HS	4.1	5.4	5.5	6.5	4.0	4.9
Graduate	4.3	7.1	5.0	4.2	2.7	5.0
Lab Force Status						
Working	4.9	9.3	9.5	8.9	7.7	7.9
Not working	1.0	0.8	1.7	1.5	0.9	1.2
Not in labor force	0.7	0.8	0.6	1.2	0.3	0.7
Relative HH Inc						
Upper third	4.9	10.9	7.2	17.5		7.6
Middle third	2.7	2.7	7.9	6.2	2.5	5.6
Lowest third	1.1	1.7	2.0	5.5	5.3	4.5
Perspectives						
See opportunity	7.6	11.7	10.1	8.5	7.8	9.0
Know entrepreneur	7.7	11.7	10.3	9.5	7.6	9.4
Have skills	8.2	12.4	12.0	10.5	9.6	10.6
Entre ready: 0	2.5	3.7	3.1	1.0	3.1	2.7
Entre ready: 1	5.7	6.0	6.6	3.0	6.0	5.6
Entre ready: 2	11.3	11.8	9.4	9.5	9.2	9.9
Entre ready: 3	16.6	13.7	13.0	12.8	9.8	12.9
Fear of failure:Yes	6.2	5.9	7.2	6.7	5.4	5.7
Fear of failure:No	5.7	9.4	8.6	7.4	6.9	7.6
Entre good career	6.4	10.2	9.9	9.9	8.2	9.0
Entre hi status	6.0	9.4	9.9	8.8	7.7	8.4
Entre good career	6.4	10.2	9.9	9.9	8.2	9.0
Entre climate: 0	2.7	4.1	4.7	3.4	2.9	3.5
Entre climate: 1	4.3	6.9	8.7	6.5	5.3	6.3
Entre climate: 2	5.3	9.9	9.1	9.5	7.7	8.4
Entre climate: 3	7.4	11.0	10.9	9.9	8.4	9.6

all levels of daily income; those with more education are more likely to be involved in new firm creation. But among the two highest daily income groups, those with high school degrees or post high school experience are the most active; those with graduate experience are less likely to be nascent entrepreneurs.[1]

The pattern is somewhat different for those involved as new firm owners. As indicated in Table 4.8 those in the three lowest daily income groups with more education are less likely to be firm owners, those from the same income groups with less education are more likely to be new firm owners. At the highest levels of daily income there is no systematic pattern associated with educational attainment.

Labor force status has a consistent and uniform effect across all income levels for both participation as a nascent entrepreneur or new firm manager. Those working are much more likely to be involved as a nascent entrepreneur or new firm owner than those not working or not in the labor force. The differences among those identified as new firm managers probably reflects classification of this new work role as work for pay.

The effect of higher relative household income on participation as nascent entrepreneur in Table 4.7 is consistent across all daily income groups; those with access to higher household incomes are more likely to become involved, often by a ratio of three to one or more. Except for the lowest daily income group, the same patterns are in Table 4.8 for the prevalence of new firm owners; those with higher relative incomes are more likely to be new firm owners. This may reflect the profitability of their new venture. The major exceptions are those in the lowest income group, where those with the lowest relative household income are more likely to be new firm owners.

The effect of the items reflecting readiness for entrepreneurship is consistent and systematic across all daily income levels for both the prevalence of nascent entrepreneurs and new firm owners. They all have a positive effect. The combined effect is measured by creating a simple scale that counts the number of items to which a person answers "yes";

---

[1] More detailed studies of participation in business creation in advanced economies, such as the United States, have consistently found that men with advanced degrees are less likely to enter business creation compared to those with college degrees (Reynolds et al., 2004).

the scale can vary from 0 to 4. The joint effect appears to be substantial, for the prevalence of participating as a nascent entrepreneur in the lowest income group for one that responds "no" to all three items is 2.9 per 100; if they respond "yes" to three items it is 13.8 — almost a fivefold increase. Increases of this magnitude are found for all income groups and participation as both nascent entrepreneurs and new firm owners. This suggests that these features have a major impact on the decision to pursue business creation.

There is a small positive effect associated with low estimates of the impact of "fear of failure." The prevalence of nascent entrepreneurs and new firm owners is generally higher for those that say they do not expect "fear of failure" to have an impact. The only exception is related to the prevalence of new firm owners in the highest income group.

The effects of the items associated with the perception of a positive climate for entrepreneurship is similar to that of measures of readiness for entrepreneurship. Positive responses are associated with a higher prevalence of nascent entrepreneurs and new firm owners. The creation of a four point scale has the same results, positive responses to more items is associated with greater participation as a nascent entrepreneur or new firm owner. The differential, however, is somewhat less, twofold or threefold compared to a fivefold increase in the prevalence rate associated with entrepreneurial readiness.

Overall then, the effects of personal factors on participation in business creation are largely the same across all levels of daily income.

- Men's participation is equal or slightly greater than women.
- Younger adults, particularly those 25–34 years old, are most involved.
- More education is associated with more participation as nascent entrepreneurs among lower income countries; those with the graduate experience as slightly less likely to be new firm owners.
- Working full or part time is associated with higher levels of participation as nascent entrepreneurs or new firm owners.
- Except for those in the lowest daily income category, those with higher relative household incomes are more involved as nascent entrepreneurs and new firm owners.

- Readiness for entrepreneurship has a strong association with greater participation as a nascent entrepreneur or new firm owners.
- An expected impact of fear of failure is associated with slightly less participation as a nascent entrepreneur or new firm owner.
- Perception of a positive entrepreneurial climate is associated with greater participation as a nascent entrepreneur or new firm owner.

5

What Kind of Businesses?

Millions of people with diverse levels of daily income are involved in business creation, 211 million in the nascent phase and 236 million as new firm owners. But what of the businesses they are creating? What types of economic activity is emphasized? And what is the potential growth of these businesses? Are those with lower daily incomes focusing entirely on small scale agriculture, retail, and services or are they involved in a wider range of firms, including those with growth potential? Fortunately, is possible to make some headway on these issues, using the data gathered in the GEM surveys. A discussion of the shift of attention from the individual participants to the nascent ventures and new firms helps to clarity the assessment.

About half of all ventures are being initiated or managed by one person. The other half are team efforts; in these cases several individuals are expecting to share ownership of a nascent firm or are jointly managing a new firm. The average number of team members associated with a nascent venture is 1.9; the average number of owners of new firms is about 1.5. There is some variation by global region and daily income, so the estimates of nascent ventures and new firm counts by

Table 5.1.   Nascent ventures counts (1000s) by daily income and global region.

	$60–$407/day	$30–$60/day	$15–$30/day	$7.50–$15/day	$1–$7.50/day	All
Asia: Developing	427	11,802	13,420	13,066	23,762	62,478
Latin America, Caribb	3,367	2,702	2,316	4,101	569	13,054
Sub-Sahara Africa	2,300	0	1,753	3,891	4,346	12,290
Middle East, N Afric	933	1,812	2,126	1,551	657	7,080
Central, East Europe	1,453	1,046	936	45	0	3,480
N Amer, Oceania	5,130	1,995	0	0	0	7,124
West Europe, Israel	2,171	848	0	0	0	3,019
Asai: Developed	1,281	6	124	0	0	1,411
All Regions	17,061	20,211	20,674	22,655	29,334	109,936

Table 5.2.   New firm counts (1000s) by daily income and global region.

	$60–$407/day	$30–$60/day	$15–$30/day	$7.50–$15/day	$1–$7.50/day	All
Asia: Developing	1,589	20,078	23,093	18,412	36,864	100,036
Latin America, Caribb	3,647	1,396	3,545	4,987	1,003	14,577
Sub-Sahara Africa	1,286	0	732	4,371	13,569	19,957
Middle East, N Afric	871	1,564	1,367	895	88	4,786
Central, East Europe	1,841	1,505	572	21	0	3,939
N Amer, Oceania	4,033	1,013	0	0	0	5,046
West Europe, Israel	2,339	693	0	0	0	3,032
Asia: Developed	2,517	2	369	0	0	2,888
All Regions	18,122	26,250	29,679	28,685	51,524	154,261

world region and daily income in Tables 5.1 and 5.2 have been adjusted by dividing by the average number of team members.[1]

As can be seen in Table 5.1, the 211 million nascent entrepreneurs are reporting on 110 nascent ventures. Table 5.2 presents the 154 million new firms represented by the 236 million new firm owners. The 447 million individuals involved in the first two stages of the firm life cycle are representing 346 million ventures.

---

[1] As team size varies slightly by world region and daily income level, unique divisors are involved for each cell of these two tables.

The distribution across the world regions presented in Tables 5.1 and 5.2 is very similar to that for the nascent entrepreneurs and new firm owners, with the majority of the activity in developing countries associated with those in the lower levels of daily income. Over half of all ventures are found in the developing countries of Asia and over half among those in the lowest three levels of daily income. In fact, over one-third of the global activity is occurring in the two lowest income categories in the developing Asian countries. At the other extreme, the three developed regions, Western Europe, Developed Asia, and North America, Oceania are the context for about 10% of the nascent ventures and 7% of the new firms. This reaffirms that the majority of business creation is taking place outside the developed regions and among those with low daily incomes.

Assessing the nature and potential impact of these ventures involves attention to the economic sectors in which they will operate, as well as the potential for high levels of contributions. High potential can be assess by considering those that (1) are expected to grow, in terms of the anticipated job creation; (2) will operate in high technology sectors, (3) are expecting to have an impact on the market in which they operate, and (4) anticipate exports outside the country.

5.1 Economic Sectors

The nature of the economic sectors emphasized by nascent ventures in each global region by daily income level is presented in Table 5.3 and for new firms in Table 5.4. The four sectors utilized in this description are:

- Extractive: All farming, forestry, fishing, and mining, including oil production.
- Transformative: Any activity that involves physical transformation of any object, such as construction, manufacturing, transportation, utilities, motor vehicle related and wholesale distribution.
- Business Services: All finance, insurance, real estate, consulting, administrative and business services.

- Consumer oriented: Any activity providing direct service to consumers, such as restaurants, bars, retail, consumer services, entertainment, recreation, religious, and health, education, and social services.

More precise classifications are precluded by the small number of cases in many countries included in the analysis.[2]

As can be seen in Tables 5.3 and 5.4, almost all sectors are represented in almost every daily income/global region category where there are nascent ventures, with the exception of an absence of extractive ventures among those below the highest daily income level in the developed Asian region. As might be expected, the consumer oriented sector is the most prominent sector in all regions and daily income levels, save for Western, Central Europe, where the transformative sectors has a slightly greater emphasis.

The bottom set of rows in Tables 5.3 and 5.4 presents a comparison across daily income groups, which make clear that the major differences are associated with a much higher proportion of extractive activity, mostly related to farming, among the two lowest daily income groups. About 15% and 19% of all nascent ventures and 18% and 16% of new firms in these groups are involved in the extractive sector. This is offset among the two highest daily income groups by a much higher proportion of business services nascent ventures. About 21% and 17% of all nascent ventures and 20% and 16% of new firms in the two highest income groups are in business services. Business service nascent ventures are particularly prevalent among the high daily income groups in the Western Europe, Israel and the North American, Oceania regions. An extractive emphasis is particularly high among the lower daily income groups of Central, Eastern Europe, MENA, and Sub-Sahara Africa regions. There is much less emphasis on extractive in the Latin American, Caribbean and developing Asian countries, which may reflect a reduction in emphasis on agriculture in these regions.

---

[2] All ventures in the GEM data set are coded using the United Nations (1990), ISIC, Revision 3; details of coding are in Reynolds (2011, p. 28).

Table 5.3. Nascent venture economic sector by global region and daily income.

Global Regions	Sectors	$60–UP/ day(%)	$30–$60/ day(%)	$15–$30/ day(%)	$7.5–$15/ day(%)	$1–7.50/ day(%)	All
Asia: Developing	Extract	4	2	3	5	6	4
	Transform	20	30	29	34	32	29
	Buss Serv	10	11	9	7	6	9
	Cons Orie	66	56	60	55	55	58
		100	100	100	100	100	100
L America, Carib	Extract	4	4	5	4	7	5
	Transform	25	24	29	25	33	27
	Buss Serv	15	11	9	5	10	10
	Cons Orie	57	61	57	65	50	58
		100	100	100	100	100	100
Sub-Sahara Africa	Extract	2	—	2	11	23	14
	Transform	20	—	25	18	18	19
	Buss Serv	15	—	7	4	0	4
	Cons Orie	62	—	66	67	59	63
		100	—	100	100	100	100
Mid East, N Afric	Extract	2	5	7	7	24	13
	Transform	30	27	19	33	8	19
	Buss Serv	7	17	13	5	17	13
	Cons Orie	62	51	61	55	50	54
		100	100	100	100	100	100
Central, E Europe	Extract	6	10	14	44	—	22
	Transform	40	38	42	29	—	36
	Buss Serv	16	13	11	6	—	11
	Cons Orie	38	39	33	21	—	31
		100	100	100	100	—	100
N Amer, Oceania	Extract	5	4	—	—	—	5
	Transform	25	25	—	—	—	25
	Buss Serv	30	24	—	—	—	27
	Cons Orie	40	47	—	—	—	43
		100	100	—	—	—	100
W Europe, Israel	Extract	3	6	—	—	—	4
	Transform	26	25	—	—	—	25
	Buss Serv	28	22	—	—	—	25
	Cons Orie	43	48	—	—	—	45
		100	100	—	—	—	100
Asia: Developed	Extract	2	0	0	—	—	1
	Transform	23	16	27	—	—	23
	Buss Serv	20	4	9	—	—	12
	Cons Orie	55	80	65	—	—	64
		100	100	100	—	—	100
All Regions	Extract	4	4	5	15	19	9
	Transform	26	26	28	25	20	25
	Buss Serv	21	17	9	5	7	13
	Cons Orie	50	53	58	55	54	54
		100	100	100	0	0	100

Table 5.4.   New firms economic sector by global region and daily income.

Global Regions	Sectors	$60–UP/ day(%)	$30–$60/ day(%)	$15–$30/ day(%)	$7.5–$15/ day(%)	$1–7.50/ day(%)	All
Asia: Developing	Extract	1	2	3	4	6	2
	Transform	20	30	69	21	23	28
	Buss Serv	7	7	14	7	3	7
	Cons Orie	71	61	14	68	68	62
		100	100	100	100	100	100
L America, Caribb	Extract	4	8	7	4	6	6
	Transform	34	25	62	31	35	37
	Buss Serv	13	14	16	6	5	10
	Cons Orie	49	52	16	58	54	47
		100	100	100	100	100	100
Sub-Sahara Africa	Extract	4	—	20	11	14	13
	Transform	29	—	42	27	26	27
	Buss Serv	15	—	19	6	1	4
	Cons Orie	52	—	19	56	58	57
		100	—	100	100	100	100
Mid East, N Afric	Extract	2	6	14	15	74	27
	Transform	36	35	54	25	10	30
	Buss Serv	15	25	16	7	0	12
	Cons Orie	47	35	16	52	16	31
		100	100	100	100	100	100
Central, East Europe	Extract	6	10	36	64	—	28
	Transform	45	38	46	8	—	31
	Buss Serv	16	9	9	0	—	9
	Cons Orie	33	43	9	28	—	32
		100	100	100	100	—	100
N Amer, Oceania	Extract	7	11	—	—	—	8
	Transform	31	26	—	—	—	29
	Buss Serv	28	21	—	—	—	26
	Cons Orie	34	42	—	—	—	37
		100	100	—	—	—	100
West Europe, Israel	Extract	4	10	—	—	—	6
	Transform	29	26	—	—	—	28
	Buss Serv	32	23	—	—	—	29
	Cons Orie	35	41	—	—	—	37
		100	100	—	—	—	100
Asia: Developed	Extract	1	0	0	—	—	1
	Transform	28	17	63	—	—	39
	Buss Serv	22	17	19	—	—	21
	Cons Orie	49	67	19	—	—	40
		100	100	100	—	—	100
All Regions	Extract	4	8	9	18	16	11
	Transform	31	29	60	25	27	31
	Buss Serv	20	16	16	5	2	11
	Cons Orie	45	48	16	53	55	47
		100	100	100	0	0	100

Aside from these general patterns, it would appear that nascent ventures are being developed in all economic sectors across all global regions and at all income levels.

5.2   Job Growth

There has been considerable attention to high potential or high growth new firms, those that are considered to be a major source of job creation. One indicator of "growth intentions" would be the number of jobs anticipated in 5 years for both nascent ventures and new firms. The number and prevalence of such growth firms by daily income is presented in Table 5.5 for both nascent ventures and new firms.

Among the 111 million nascent ventures about 12 million, or 11%, expect to have over 20 employees in 5 years. About 10 million, or 6%, of the new firms expect to have over 20 employees in the next 5 years. The prevalence among the adult human population is quite low; about 0.3 per 100 for growth oriented nascent ventures and about 0.2 per 100 adults for growth oriented new firms. It is clear that for both stages of business creation, growth oriented ventures are concentrated among those with higher levels of daily income. About 57% of growth oriented nascent ventures and 66% of growth oriented new firms are among those in the highest two levels of daily income.

Table 5.5.   Job growth oriented nascent ventures and new firms by daily income (Expecting 20 or more jobs 5 years after start-up).

Daily income	Number of adults, 18–64 years old (millions)	Prevalence [#/100] of growth oriented nascent ventures	Number of growth oriented nascent ventures (millions)	Percent	Prevalence [#/100] of growth oriented new firms	Number of growth oriented new firms (millions)	Percent
$60–$407	830	0.25	2.1	17.0	0.25	2.1	21.8
$30–$60	733	0.67	4.9	39.7	0.57	4.2	44.1
$15–$30	832	0.27	2.2	18.2	0.16	1.3	14.1
$7.50–$15	737	0.13	1.0	7.8	0.12	0.9	9.1
$1–$7.50	1,116	0.19	2.1	17.3	0.09	1.3	10.8
Total	4,248	0.29	12.3	100.0	0.22	9.5	99.9

Table 5.6.   Job growth nascent ventures counts (1,000) by daily income and global region.

	$60–$407/ day	$30–$60/ day	$15–$30/ day	$7.50–$15/ day	$1–$7.50/ day	All
Asia: Developing	29	4,069	1,635	438	1,773	7,944
Latin America, Caribb	336	137	194	159	76	901
Sub-Sahara Africa	119	—	132	160	260	670
Middle East, N Afric	335	284	212	206	27	1,064
Central, East Europe	216	110	49	1	—	376
N Amer, Oceania	698	237	—	—	—	936
West Europe, Israel	217	60	—	—	—	278
Asia: Developed	144	1	21	—	—	166
All Regions	2,094	4,898	2,243	964	2,135	12,334

Table 5.7.   Job growth new firm counts (1,000) by daily income and global region.

	$60–$407/ day	$30–$60/ day	$15–$30/ day	$7.50–$15/ day	$1–$7.50/ day	All
Asia: Developing	80	3,853	1,022	490	604	6,048
Latin America, Caribb	300	51	166	107	53	677
Sub-Sahara Africa	106	—	33	153	376	668
Middle East, N Afric	129	102	81	119	0	430
Central, East Europe	259	107	39	0	—	405
N Amer, Oceania	645	69	—	—	—	715
West Europe, Israel	282	29	—	—	—	311
Asia: Developed	278	0	8	—	—	286
All Regions	2,078	4,212	1,348	869	1,033	9,539

The actual counts by world region, however, provide a more nuanced description. These are provided by income level and global region in Table 5.6 for nascent ventures and Table 5.7 for new firms.

Over 60% of the activity is in the developing Asian countries; one-third is in developing Asian regions among those in the second from the top daily income category. There is a considerable presence of high growth ventures and new firms in the other developing regions, although mostly among the higher daily income categories.

This overview make clear that while those in higher daily income categories are more likely to pursue high job growth with their ventures and firms, those in the lower daily income categories are a substantial part of world population of growth oriented nascent ventures and new firms.

5.3   High Technology

High technology sectors have been identified as those with a relatively high proportion of employees with scientific, engineering, or technological training. This has been done for the U.S. Standard Industrial Classification System and applied to the economic sectors of the GEM nascent ventures and new firms.[3] As a criterion for identifying a high technology emphasis, this is only partially successful, for many of the firms in these sectors are not engaged in substantial research and development. Nevertheless, this provides a basis for estimating the number of nascent ventures in high technology sectors. This is done by daily income category for nascent ventures and new firms in Table 5.8. Note that the overall prevalence of 0.47 per 100 is higher for nascent ventures than the prevalence of 0.24 per 100 for new firms.

As can be seen in Table 5.8, those from higher daily income categories are more likely to be associated with nascent ventures and new firms in high technology sectors. Even so, those in the two bottom daily income categories are responsible for more than a third of both nascent ventures and new firms in high technology sectors.

The number of nascent ventures and new firms in high tech sectors for different world regions and income levels is presented in Tables 5.9

Table 5.8.   Nascent ventures and new firms in high tech sectors by daily income.

Daily income	Number of adults, 18–64 years old (millions)	Prevalence [#/100] of high tech sector nascent ventures	Number of high tech sector nascent ventures (millions)	Percent	Prevalence [#/100] of high tech sector new firms	Number of high tech sector new firms (millions)	Percent
$60–$407	830	0.42	3.4	17.6	0.25	2.1	20.5
$30–$60	733	0.62	4.6	23.2	0.29	2.1	20.9
$15–$30	832	0.52	4.3	21.9	0.28	2.3	23.2
$7.50–$15	737	0.40	3.0	15.0	0.24	1.8	17.4
$1–$7.50	1,116	0.39	4.4	22.3	0.16	1.8	18.0
Total	4,248	0.47	19.8	100.0	0.24	9.5	100.0

---

[3] This procedure was implemented by Hecker (2005); a summary of the high technology sectors is provided in Appendix B of Reynolds (2011).

Table 5.9.   High tech sector nascent ventures counts (1,000s) by daily income and global region.

	$60–$407/ day	$30–$60/ day	$15–$30/ day	$7.50–$15/ day	$1–$7.50/ day	All
Asia: Developing	91	3,425	3,537	1,975	4,139	13,168
Latin America, Caribb	553	360	285	447	104	1,749
Sub-Sahara Africa	242	—	152	315	151	860
Middle East, N Afric	113	230	180	219	5	747
Central, East Europe	318	142	163	13	—	636
N Amer, Oceania	1,128	274	—	—	—	1,401
West Europe, Israel	619	149	—	—	—	768
Asia: Developed	418	1	18	—	—	437
All Regions	3,481	4,581	4,336	2,970	4,400	19,768

Table 5.10.   High tech sector new firms counts (1,000s) by daily income and global region.

	$60–$407/ day	$30–$60/ day	$15–$30/ day	$7.50–$15/ day	$1–$7.50/ day	All
Asia: Developing	126	1,520	1,698	945	1,493	5,782
Latin America, Caribb	366	128	315	425	39	1,272
Sub-Sahara Africa	131	—	59	274	277	741
Middle East, N Afric	88	167	186	109	2	551
Central, East Europe	193	116	42	3	—	354
N Amer, Oceania	463	108	—	—	—	572
West Europe, Israel	382	67	—	—	—	450
Asia: Developed	318	0	42	—	—	360
All Regions	2,067	2,107	2,342	1,757	1,811	10,083

and 5.10. The dominance of the developing Asian countries, where 67% of nascent ventures and 57% of new firms in high tech sectors are located, is striking. This is more than three times the number in the three developed regions, Western Europe, Israel, North America, Oceania, and developed Asia, which have 13% of the nascent ventures and 15% of the new firms in high technology sectors.

There is no question, from this assessment, that those with low daily incomes are a significant minority of those pursuing business creation in high tech sectors, mostly in the developing Asian countries.

5.4   Market Impact

The potential impact of new businesses on markets has been empha-sized by the image of "creative destruction." This emphasizes the changes in the market structure (new products, new production processes, and the like) that can occur when new firms are implemented.[4] Three questions were utilized in the GEM interviews to identify the expected impact of the firm on the market in which they compete. Those that reported no competitors, customers unfamiliar with the product or service, and the use of new technology were assumed to have a high level of impact on the market. Those that reported many competitors, customers that knew their product or service very well, and the use of old technology was assumed to have little impact on the markets. Based on the index created from these items, nascent ventures or new firms expecting any market impact can be identified.

The interpretation of this index can vary depending on the context. A firm creating a dramatic new computer gadget or software program for sale over the internet to the global information technology market may have a different response to the items than a new firm in rural India that provides, for the first time, mobile phones to those within a 50 kilometer radius. Both may report they expect to have a major market impact, but their markets are dramatically different and the "newness" of their product, in an absolute sense, may be quite different.

The prevalence and number of nascent ventures and new firms expecting any market impact is presented in Table 5.11. About 40 million nascent ventures, 36% of the total, and 48 million new firms, 31%

Table 5.11.   Nascent ventures and new firms expecting market impact by daily income.

Daily income	Number of adults, 18–64 years old (millions)	Prevalence [#/100] of market impact nascent ventures	Number of market impact nascent ventures (millions)	Percent	Prevalence [#/100] of market impact new firms	Number of high market impact new firms (millions)	Percent
$60–$407	830	0.78	6.4	16.2	0.69	5.7	12.0
$30–$60	733	1.13	8.2	20.8	1.20	8.8	18.5
$15–$30	832	0.87	7.3	18.3	0.94	7.8	16.5
$7.50–$15	737	1.05	7.8	19.5	1.25	9.2	19.3
$1–$7.50	1,116	0.90	10.0	25.2	1.44	16.0	33.7
Total	4,248	0.94	39.7	100.0	1.12	47.5	100.0

---

[4] Schumpeter (1934).

Table 5.12. Market impact nascent venture counts (1,000s) by daily income and global region.

	$60–$407/ day	$30–$60/ day	$15–$30/ day	$7.50–$15/ day	$1–$7.50/ day	All
Asia: Developing	200	4,525	4,362	3,868	8,334	21,289
Latin America, Caribb	1,347	1,313	858	1,521	260	5,299
Sub-Sahara Africa	1,058	—	747	1,617	984	4,407
Middle East, N Afric	469	826	1,067	728	420	3,510
Central, East Europe	319	345	203	16	—	883
N Amer, Oceania	1,766	862	—	—	—	2,628
West Europe, Israel	897	379	—	—	—	1,276
Asia: Developed	393	2	38	—	—	433
All Regions	6,450	8,252	7,275	7,750	9,999	39,726

Table 5.13. Market impact new firm counts (1,000s) by daily income and global region.

	$60–$407/ day	$30–$60/ day	$15–$30/ day	$7.50–$15/ day	$1–$7.50/ day	All
Asia: Developing	771	6,814	5,917	6,389	13,317	33,209
Latin America, Caribb	1,096	443	893	1,225	363	4,020
Sub-Sahara Africa	575	—	299	1,192	2,312	4,378
Middle East, N Afric	343	698	513	364	27	1,945
Central,East Europe	461	273	120	8	—	862
N Amer, Oceania	1,195	353	—	—	—	1,548
West Europe, Israel	724	225	—	—	—	949
Asia: Developed	547	0	90	—	—	638
All Regions	5,713	8,806	7,832	9,178	16,018	47,548

of the total, expect to have some impact on their markets. Over 40% of the nascent ventures and over 50% of the new firms expecting a market impact are associated with the two lowest daily income categories.

The distribution of firms expecting a market impact by global regions and daily income is provided in Table 5.12 for nascent ventures and Table 5.13 for new firms.

As almost all those with low daily income live in developing countries, the high concentration of market impact nascent ventures and new firms in this region is to be expected. In fact, 78% of the market impact nascent ventures and 86% of the market impact new firms are in three developing regions of Asia, Latin America, Caribbean, and sub-Sahara Africa. Many of these firms are, no doubt, having an impact in very local markets.

5.5 Exports

The emphasis on exports is determined by asking about the expected, for nascent ventures, or current, for operating firms, proportion of customers that would normally reside outside the country. This wording allows sales to tourists to be considered an export of a travel experience. Those expecting any (1% or more) of their customers to live outside the country are considered to have an export emphasis. The proportion of nascent ventures and new firms with export potential or activity is shown in Table 5.14.

The proportion of export activity is relatively low, as only 13 million, or 12% of nascent ventures, and 10 million, or 6% of new firms, report any customers living outside their country. The relative contribution of nascent ventures (44% of the total) and new firms (21%) in the two lowest income categories is modest, but significant.

The patterns of nascent ventures and new firms expecting exports by global region and daily income level are presented in Tables 5.15 and 5.16. It helps to clarity this pattern.

Nascent ventures or new firms in small countries that wish to expand sales have little choice but to pursue customers abroad. Ventures and firms with large domestic markets, such as those in China, India, Brazil, the United States, Russia, Japan, or Indonesia, can grow to considerable size without any exports. As a result, world regions composed of a large number of smaller countries may be expected to have more

Table 5.14. Nascent ventures and new firms expecting exports by daily income.

Daily income	Number of adults, 18–64 years old (millions)	Prevalence [#/100] of export activity nascent ventures	Number of export activity nascent ventures (millions)	Percent	Prevalence [#/100] of export activity new firms	Number of export activity new firms (millions)	Percent
$60–$407	830	0.43	3.6	27.4	0.33	2.7	28.9
$30–$60	733	0.03	0.2	1.9	0.36	2.6	27.9
$15–$30	832	0.43	3.5	27.0	0.25	2.1	21.8
$7.50–$15	737	0.35	2.6	19.7	0.16	1.2	12.6
$1–$7.50	1,116	0.28	3.1	24.1	0.07	0.8	8.7
Total	4,248	0.31	13.1	100.1	0.22	9.5	99.9

Table 5.15.   Nascent ventures expecting exports counts (1,000s) by daily income and global region.

	$60–$407/ day	$30–$60/ day	$15–$30/ day	$7.50–$15/ day	$1–$7.50/ day	All
Asia: Developing	71	113	2,283	997	2,593	6,057
Latin America, Caribb	483	27	236	312	56	1,113
Sub-Sahara Africa	785	—	498	856	388	2,527
Middle East, N Afric	200	37	369	406	131	1,143
Central, East Europe	329	13	141	14	—	497
N Amer, Oceania	838	32	—	—	—	871
West Europe, Israel	648	22	—	—	—	670
Asia: Developed	244	0	21	—	—	266
All Regions	3,599	244	3,548	2,585	3,168	13,144

Table 5.16.   New firms expecting exports counts (1,000s) by daily income and global region.

	$60–$407/ day	$30–$60/ day	$15–$30/ day	$7.50–$15/ day	$1–$7.50/ day	All
Asia: Developing	121	1,953	1,303	501	510	4,388
Latin America, Caribb	335	96	169	165	63	828
Sub-Sahara Africa	432	—	140	451	241	1,264
Middle East, N Afric	116	208	320	74	8	726
Central, East Europe	217	118	76	5	—	416
N Amer, Oceania	585	110	—	—	—	695
West Europe, Israel	561	157	—	—	—	718
Asia: Developed	372	1	57	—	—	430
All Regions	2,740	2,643	2,065	1,196	822	9,466

ventures and firms with an export orientation than regions with a small number of large countries. As the countries with the largest domestic populations are in the developed Asian region, this may be the reason for the relative low number expecting export activity, compared to the numbers in high tech sectors or expecting a market impact.

It is clear, however, that nascent ventures and new firms associated with low daily income provide a significant proportion of export activity.

The 211 million nascent entrepreneurs are involved in launching about 110 million nascent ventures; the 236 million new firm owners are managing 154 million new firms. Those with daily incomes of less than $15 are associated with 46 million nascent ventures and 80 million new firms. These initiatives, implemented by the poor, are:

- Operating in all economic sectors, albeit with a smaller proportion in business services compared to those with the highest daily income.
- Include 3 million nascent ventures and 2 million new firms expecting to create 20 or more jobs in 5 years.
- Include 7 million nascent ventures and 4 million new firms in high technology sectors.
- Include 18 million nascent ventures and 25 million new firms expecting to have some impact on the markets in which they compete.
- Include 6 million nascent ventures and 3 million new firms expecting to serve customers living outside their countries.

In summary, the firms implemented by the bottom billion are involved in all economic sectors and are a significant proportion, albeit a minority, of those ventures and firms making distinctive contributions.

6

Jobs and Job Creation

There is much evidence to suggest that job creation is associated with economic growth and renewal. In most growth economies there is a substantial churning among firms and jobs, and continuous job creation by new firms is a major source of replacing the jobs lost from firm shrinkage and closures. Given the active role of the poor as nascent entrepreneurs and new firm owners it is possible to consider their contributions to the job creation process. New firms also provide an economic role for the owners, and the average new firm has about two owners. Job counts, then, include both owner-managers and employees. Job counts will be based on those reported by profitable firms at the time of the interview, not future expectations.

Exploring the role of firms managed by those with different daily household incomes is a two step process. First is a consideration, by global region, of the sources of jobs provided by all private sector firms. Second is an assessment of jobs provided by new firms, those that have been profitable for up to three and a half years. These firms are as major sources of new jobs. Estimates of the global counts of firms and

Table 6.1.   Total firms and jobs by global region.

Global region	Adults:18–64 yrs old (1,000)	Firms (1,000)	Jobs (1,000)	Firms/100 Adults	Jobs/100 Adults	Unemployment: 2000–2008 (%)	Gov. Jobs/All Jobs: 2005 (%)
Asia: Developing	2,265,552	352,753	1,327,907	15.6	58.6	4.7	7.1
Latin America, Caribb	346,200	43,086	125,581	12.4	36.3	8.5	9.7
Sub-Sahara Africa	438,596	47,329	160,554	10.8	36.6	19.5	9.6
Middle East, N Afric	249,670	18,954	98,440	7.6	39.4	11.1	17.4
Central, East Europe	322,774	12,790	113,208	4.0	35.1	9.9	26.2
N Amer, Oceania	232,513	18,631	155,727	8.0	67.0	5.3	14.6
West Europe, Israel	262,469	16,277	120,562	6.2	45.9	7.7	18.7
Asia: Developed	132,271	12,396	109,407	9.4	82.7	4.4	10.5
Total/Average	4,250,046	522,216	2,211,386	9.2	50.2	8.9	14.2

jobs were developed following procedures similar to those for producing estimates of those at different levels of daily income.[1]

A summary of the overall results is provided in Table 6.1 for each global region.

The second column lists the number of midlife adults, those 18–24 years of age. The third column indicates that a global total of 522

---

[1] A number of adjustments were involved in the analysis. (1) As a very small proportion, less than 1%, of new and established ventures reported large number of owners, perhaps reflecting a large number of investors, ownership teams with more than ten members were reset to ten. (2) A small proportion, less than 0.4%, of nascent and existing firms reported current employment in the thousands, the largest was 700,000. When the median employment is less than 5, these extreme outliers can have dramatic effects on the average values. To minimize these distortions, cases with employment in excess of 500 employees was reset to 500. (3) Global region estimates were created by estimating the prevalence for the sample of countries from each region, weighted to reflect their proportion of the midlife adult population in the region, and multiplying this by the total population of midlife adults in the region. (4) As firms with more owners were more likely to be included in the survey, the initial estimates of survey counts was divided by the average number of owners for each region and level of daily income. (5) Job estimates were produced by multiplying the estimated prevalence of firms by the average number of total jobs (owners and employees, determined for each level of daily income in each region). Due to missing data on new firms, Yemen was excluded from the analysis.

million firms are in operation providing, as shown in column four, 2.2 billion jobs. Note that the GEM screening procedure will not capture two major sources of employment, government agencies and that provided by extremely large corporations, public, private, and family owned. These latter firms are a major course of private employment. In the United States, and other advanced economies, these mega-firms are a fraction of a percent of the total but account for about half of all employment. The World Economic Forum, representing the interests of global corporations, restricts its membership to one thousand of the largest global firms. Hence, the firm and job counts can be considered to represent the world wide activity of micro, small, and medium sized firms, but not the massive multi-nationals or government agencies.

The fourth column in Table 6.1 indicates that 2.2 billion jobs have been associated with these 500 million firms. The ratio of firms and jobs to the midlife adult population is presented in columns five and six. As a basis for comparison column seven presents the average unemployment rate from 2000 to 2008 and column eight the proportion of all workers that are government employees in 2005.[2]

There are no major inconsistencies to suggest that the overall patterns are not reasonable. The lowest prevalence of jobs, 35 per 100 midlife adults, in central and Eastern Europe occurs where there is a high proportion of government workers, 26%, who would not be included in these estimates, the unemployment rate slightly above average, and there is a very low firm prevalence, 4 per 100 adults, suggesting that large organizations would be a major source of jobs. In contrast, high prevalence of jobs, 83 per 100 adults, is found in developed Asian countries, where there is a low ratio of government employees, a low unemployment rate, and a high firm prevalence rate of 9 per 100 adults, suggesting an economy with a high proportion of smaller firms. This would suggest that the assessment provides a reasonable first approximation of the global distribution of firms and jobs.

The distribution of firms by global region and the owner's daily income is provided in Figure 6.1; the distribution of jobs is provided in Figure 6.2.

---

[2] Details on the sources of these two measures are in Reynolds (2011).

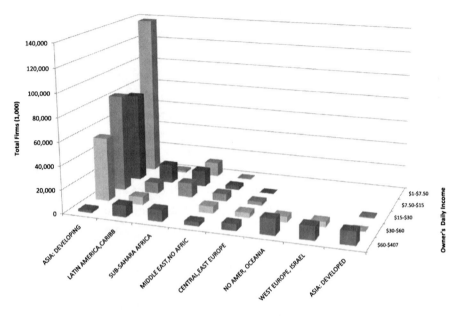

Fig. 6.1 Total firms by owner's daily income and global region.

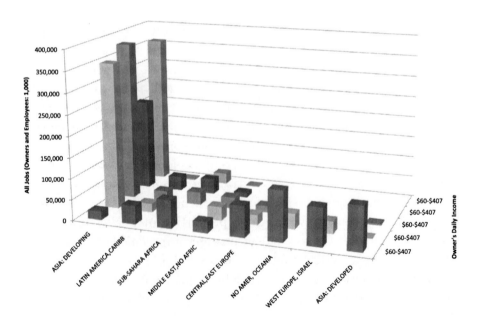

Fig. 6.2 Total jobs by firm owner's daily income and global region.

There are major differences in the patterns for the different global regions. The three high national income regions (North America, Oceania; Western Europe, Israel; and Developed Asia) have a high proportion of firms owned by those with the highest daily incomes, in excess of $60 per day. Complementing this pattern, the largest proportion of jobs in these three global regions is associated with firms where the owners have the highest daily income. Those with the highest daily income account for 68 million or 13% of all firms providing 547 million or 25% of all jobs.

In contrast, while the developing regions (Sub-Sahara Africa, Latin America, and, in particular, developing Asia) have some firms and employment associated with owners in the highest daily incomes, these are a minority of the firms and employment. By far the largest proportion of firms, and jobs, are owned by those with the lowest daily incomes. Those with daily incomes less than $15 per day are associated with 260 million firms, half of the total, providing 691 million jobs or 31% of the total. The bar charts help illustrate the dominance of the developing Asian countries (which includes China and India) as a context for firms and jobs associated with low daily income owners.

Two regions are intermediate between these two extremes. Both the Middle East North African and Central and Eastern Europe are intermediate between the lowest and highest national income groups. In both regions the presence of firms and jobs is more evenly distributed across owners in all daily income categories.

New firms create new jobs. The current jobs created by new firms, those in profit for up to three and a half years, can be considered new jobs. The number of new firms by the daily income of the owners for each global region is presented in Figure 6.3; the jobs they have created, which includes both those for the owners as well as employees, is provided in Figure 6.4.

The role of those with low daily income is similar to their role among all existing firms. Those with daily income of $1–$15 per day are responsible for about half, 48% or 86 million, of the new firms providing 32% or 234 million new jobs for themselves and others — mostly others. Those with the highest daily income, $60 or more per day, are associated with 13% of the new firms and 23% of the new firm jobs.

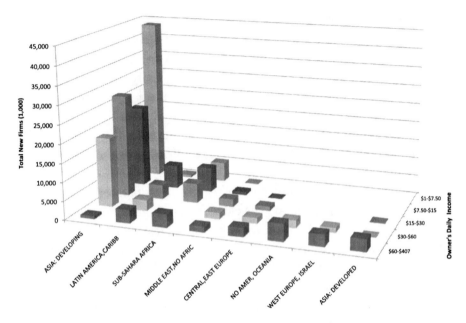

Fig. 6.3 Total new firms by owner's daily income and global region.

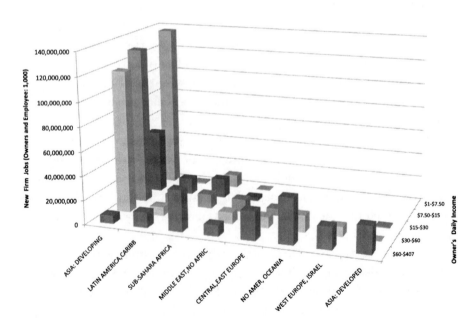

Fig. 6.4 Total new firm jobs by owner's daily income and global region.

In the four regions with the highest GDP per Capita, firms owned by those with the highest daily income, greater than $60 per day, provide 60% or more of the new firm jobs. In three of the developing regions, Developing Asia; Latin America, Caribbean, and MENA, firms owned by those in the intermediate levels of daily income, from $7.50 to $60, are the sources of seven in ten new jobs. Sub-Sahara Africa appears unique in the role of firms with the highest daily income, a source of one in five new jobs, as well as the very lowest levels, below $15 per day, a source of three in five jobs. This may, again, reflect the high level of income disparity in sub-Sahara Africa.

The relative contributions within each global region highlight major differences. The proportion of new firms by owner's daily income for each region is provided in Table 6.2 and the proportion of jobs in Table 6.3. There are dramatic differences between the rich and developing countries. About seven in ten new firms in the advanced country regions (North America, Oceania; Western Europe, Israel; and Developed Asia) are associated with high daily income owners, compared to less than one in four in the developing regions (Developing Asia, Latin America, Caribbean, Sub-Sahara Africa, and MENA). As a result, over half of the jobs in the developing countries are provided by owners with daily incomes below $30 per day, and one in three jobs in Developing Asia, Latin America, and Sub-Sahara Africa are provided by new firm owners with daily income less than $15 per day.

Table 6.2. Percentage of new firms by owner's daily income by each global region.

	$60–$407 (%)	$30–$60 (%)	$15–$30 (%)	$7.50–$15 (%)	$1–$7.50 (%)	Row total (%)
Asia: Developing	0.7	16.6	24.5	19.4	38.9	100.0
Latin America, Caribb	20.6	16.7	22.3	36.7	3.8	100.0
Sub-Sahara Africa	17.4	—	25.2	31.9	25.5	100.0
Middle East, N Afric	24.4	27.2	33.0	13.5	1.9	100.0
Central,East Europe	47.7	29.4	22.6	0.3	—	100.0
N Amer, Oceania	69.8	30.2	—	—	—	100.0
West Europe, Israel	70.9	29.1	—	—	—	100.0
Asia: Developed	94.1	1.1	4.8	—	—	100.0
All Regions	13.1	15.9	22.6	20.2	28.1	100.0

Table 6.3.   Percentage of new firm jobs by owner's daily income by each global region.

	$60–$407 (%)	$30–$60 (%)	$15–$30 (%)	$7.50–$15 (%)	$1–$7.50 (%)	Row total (%)
Asia: Developing	1.5	26.6	29.3	11.7	30.8	100.0
Latin America, Caribb	29.5	17.1	19.5	31.2	2.7	100.0
Sub-Sahara Africa	47.0	—	16.2	21.9	14.9	100.0
Middle East, N Afric	28.2	29.1	32.5	9.3	1.0	100.0
Central, East Europe	61.1	23.2	15.5	0.2	—	100.0
N Amer, Oceania	73.0	27.0	—	—	—	100.0
West Europe, Israel	69.5	30.5	—	—	—	100.0
Asia: Developed	96.0	0.6	3.4	—	—	100.0
All regions	22.6	22.7	22.9	11.5	20.3	100.0

Several conclusions are justified by this global assessment of the sources of firms and jobs:

- The GEM adult population surveys provide a useful first approximation of the global scope of firms and jobs provided by firms owned by those with different daily incomes.
- Those with low daily incomes, below $15 per day, are managing half of the global estimate of 522 million firms providing one-third of the global estimate of 2.2 billion jobs.
- Those with low daily incomes, below $15 per day, are the source of one half of all new firms and one-third of all new jobs worldwide, and as much as 40% in developing, low income countries.

Without the contributions of those from low income households to the firm and job creation process, the economic plight of the bottom billions would be even more severe.

7

National Factors, Individual Attributes, and Business Creation

It is widely recognized that individual behavior is affected by personal attributes and contextual factors. Sorting out the relative impact has long been a major theme in social science. Entire disciplines have emphasized different approaches. A major focus of psychology is on using enduring personal attributes to predict future individual attitudes and behavior. A major emphasis of sociology, as well as anthropology, is on the role of group, societal, or cultural factors in guiding, or constraining, individual behavior. Much economic analysis has given attention to the impact of context, or macro-economic conditions, on national economic growth. There is also a focus on how individuals actually respond in different situations.

One approach to defining the context for individual behavior makes a distinction between formal and informal institutions.

> Institutions are the humanly devised constraints that structure human interaction. They are made up of formal constraints (rules, laws, constitutions), informal constraints (norms of behavior, conventions, and self-imposed codes of conduct), and their enforcement

characteristics. Together they define the incentive structure of societies and specifically economies.[1]

In most cases formal and informal institutions complement each other.
It can be assumed that both types of institutions emerge over time as
a consequence of "societal learning." The formal structures — con-
stitutions, laws, programs — often reflect well established informal
institutions. The following assessment involves many national factors
representing the formal and informal institutions associated with this
conceptualization. In particular, two aspects of national values reflect
significant aspects of informal institutions.

While new businesses are the product of deliberate efforts by
individuals or teams, it is clear that in some contexts there is more business creation than in others. On the other hand, in all economies only
a minority pursue new firm creation. Estimating the relative impact of
national characteristics, formal and informal institutions, and personal
attributes on participation in business creation is one of the major
challenges in understanding the entrepreneurial process. The greater
challenge, of course, is to establish the mechanisms that link national
factors to individual behavior.

This has considerable implications for public policy. If the major
factors affecting business creation were individual attributes, then
policies should focus on individual selection or training. If the major
factors were contextual in nature, then policies should focus on adjusting national institutions, either the formal structures or the informal
milieu. The most likely outcome, of course, is that both individual
attributes and national factors have an effect. In that case, the emphasis
shifts to the relative impact of each and, in addition, which specific individual attributes and national factors are having an impact. National
factors also vary in terms of which can be affected by government
action. For example, there is substantial evidence that young adults,
in their twenties, are most active in firm creation. More young adults,

---

[1] North (1993) based on North (1990). This is distinct from the efforts to explain the presence of productive organizations, where an administrative component coordinates the work
of a group of people, as a response to the inefficiencies of coordinating economic production with a price based market mechanism, frequently described as the "new institutional
economics" (Coase, 1937; Hodgson, 1998; Williamson, 2000).

then, should lead to more firm creation. But while there are isolated examples of successes in reducing the birth rates in national populations, successful government efforts to increase human birth rates are rare. Identifying national factors that can increase firm creation and can be affected by government policies is a major challenge.

Determining the potential for government action to influence business creation is facilitated by exploring all potential causal influences. Many national characteristics have been proposed as affecting the amount of indigenous business creation. These features are related to processes that will affect individual participation in entrepreneurial activity. Almost all of these processes are related to five aspects of a national economy: basic economic characteristics, structural features, measures of centralized control or regulation, capacity of the population for business creation, and national cultural and social support.

These five national aspects can be represented by 25 individual measures as follows[2]:

Economic characteristics: GDP per capita, recent increase in GDP per capita, recent population increases, and income inequality (the GINI index).

Structural features of the economy: Prevalence of established enterprises, percentage of the work force in agriculture (farming, forestry, and fishing), industry (mining, construction, manufacturing, and utilities), and services (everything else).

Centralized Control, Regulation of the Economy: The proportion of government employees in the labor force, government spending as a proportion of annual GDP, index of business registration costs, commercial legal costs index, legal recognition of physical property rights index, legal recognition of intellectual property rights index, and corruption.[3]

---

[2] Summarized in Appendix D1, detailed descriptions including procedures for estimating missing values are found in Reynolds (2011).

[3] The index represents a western conception of corruption, where those in official positions expect "side payments" to perform official duties. In societies where the most reliable sources of personal assistance or elementary justice are within trusted informal networks of family members or a tribal community, corruption is considered "the failure to share

Population Capacity for Business Creation: National index of entrepreneurial ready adults, percentage population 25–44 years old,
percent adult population with secondary school degrees, labor
force participation by men, labor force participation by women,
and the unemployment rate.

National Cultural and Social Norms: Prevalence of informal investors,
cultural support for entrepreneurship, emphasis on traditional
versus secular-rational values, and an emphasis on survival versus self-expressive values.

Virtually all of these variables are represented by continuous measures
and almost all have a statistically significant association with measures
of business creation.

Note that the formal institutional factors are reflected in the measures related to the centralized control and regulation of the economy.
Formal institutions may have an indirect effect on some aspects of
population readiness, such as the proportion of adults that complete
educational programs and the proportion of women that participate in
the labor force. In extreme case, government institutions may affect the
age structure of the population, but these efforts have had very mixed
success.

Informal institutions are reflected in the national cultural and social
norms, well represented in this selection of measures.

One version of this conceptual scheme is presented in Figure 7.1. The
box at the top left presents five categories of national factors reflected
in 25 specific measures. The box at the bottom left reflects six individual attributes with one, readiness for entrepreneurship, represented by
three indicators. The middle boxes reflect participation in the first two
stages of the firm life course, individuals involved in the start-up phase
as nascent entrepreneurs or as owner-managers of new firms. The two
boxes on the right represent the prevalence of nascent entrepreneurs or
new firm owners in the adult population, both identified as national
characteristics.

---

any largess you have received with those with whom you have formed ties of dependence"
(Rosen, 2010).

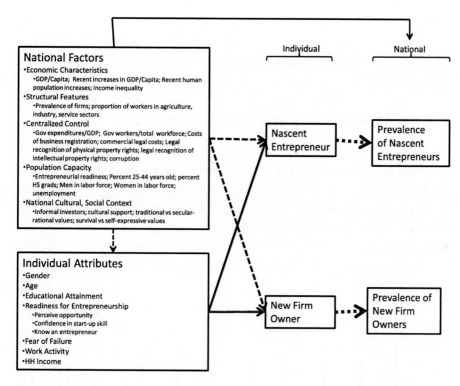

Fig. 7.1 National and individual factors affecting participation in business creation.

There is already considerable evidence related to this conceptual framework. For example, there has been substantial research on national factors affecting the prevalence of new firm creation. This is represented by the solid arrow at the top of Figure 6.1 linking national factors with measures of the prevalence of start-ups (nascent entrepreneurs) or new firms (new firm owners). An example of such an assessment follows, which indicates that models of the relationship between national factors and the level of business creation activity have a high level of predictive success.

The potential impact of national factors on individual attributes and individual participation in business creation is represented by the dashed line arrow from the national factors box. A first step in developing a more complete understanding would be to determine the relative impact of these two different levels of analysis, the individual and the national. The same problem has emerged in a wide range of other social science phenomena, which has lead to the development of multi-level modeling techniques.[4] These procedures are utilized in the assessment that follows.

7.1   National Factors and Business Creation

There is a considerable range in the national prevalence of those involved in business creation with different levels of daily income. These distributions are presented in Figure 7.2, the national prevalence for nascent entrepreneurs to the left and new firm owners to the right. The horizontal bars represent the average values; the range from low to high is represented by the vertical bars. While there is little variation in the average values, there are substantial differences in the amount

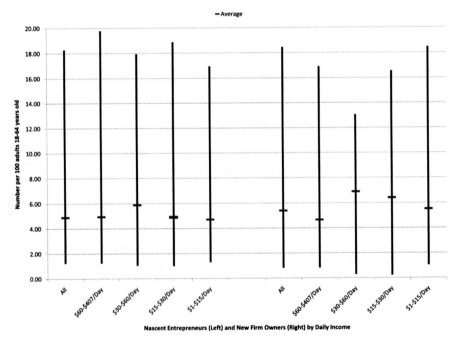

Fig. 7.2 Distribution of nascent and new firm owners national prevalance by daily income.

---

[4] Hofmann (1997), Kreft and de Leeuw (1998), Raudenbush and Bryk (2002).

of activity among those with the same level of daily income in different countries.

As seen in Figure 7.2, the range of differences in prevalence rates (the high divided by the low) varies from 10 to 19; there is at least a tenfold difference between the lowest and highest prevalence rates. This suggests that country characteristics are having a major impact on the level of participation. The substantial variation among those with the two highest daily incomes, $60–$407 and $30–$60, reflects the inclusion of many developing countries in these high income categories.[5] The high income disparity in many developing countries reflects the substantial minority with high daily incomes. Further, most distributions are somewhat lopsided, or skewed, with a larger range of values above the average represented by the horizontal bar.[6]

This substantial diversity suggests that it would be useful to explore national differences related to differences in business activity. Two assessments follow. The first uses standardized regression procedures to develop linear additive models of national characteristics to predict variation in national measures of business creation activity, the prevalence of nascent entrepreneurs and new firm owners. The second uses multi-level modeling procedures to develop linear additive models that incorporate both individual factors and national characteristics to predict national variation in business creation activity. As will be seen, both sets of models are relatively successful at predicting differences in national levels of business creation.

The five major national domains are represented by 25 specific indicators in the modeling building exercise.[7] One national characteristic is adjusted for this assessment.

Often considered an indicator of economic development, GDP per Capita has received substantial attention. Assessments of the relationship between GDP per Capita and participation in business creation have been "nonlinear."[8] The usual pattern is an inverted "U" shape,

---

[5] The countries in each daily income group are presented in Appendix F.

[6] Measures of prevalence are adjusted with a logarithmic transform to create a normal distribution for the regression modeling assessments.

[7] Sources are summarized in Appendix E.

[8] Wennekers et al. (2005), based the Total Entrepreneurial Activity (TEA) index which includes both nascent entrepreneurs and new firm owners.

with high levels of participation among the poorest countries, lowest levels among countries with intermediate levels of GDP per Capita, and slightly higher rates of participation among those with the highest levels of personal income. For this reason, GDP per Capita is represented by three dummy variables, with 38 countries in the lowest group with GDP per Capita from US\$ 1,000 to US\$ 16,000, 16 in the intermediate group with GDP per Capita between US\$ 16,000 and US\$ 35,000; and 20 in the highest group with GDP per Capita from US\$ 35,000 to US\$ 57,000.[9] The intermediate national income level was used as a base for comparison and not included as a predictor in the regression assessments.

In the current data set, the prevalence of nascent entrepreneurs is 6.5 per 100 among the low income countries, compared to 2.9 per 100 among the middle income countries and 2.7 per 100 among the high income countries, not quite a "U" shape but a pronounced "L." The prevalence of new firm owners, however, is 5.4 per 100 among the low income countries, 2.3 per 100 among the middle income countries, and 3.7 per 100 among the high income countries. This is definitely a "U-shaped" relationship.

The development of the linear additive models uses a basic regression modeling procedure.[10] As the distributions of the prevalence of nascent entrepreneurs and new firm owners are heavily skewed, a logarithmic transform is used to create normal distributions for all dependent variables. The residuals for all models approximate a normal distribution, indicating that no extreme outliers are having an undue influence on the results. In all assessments the countries were weighted

---

[9] Twenty high income countries included Australia, Austria, Belgium, Canada, Denmark, Finland, France, Germany, Hong Kong, Iceland, Ireland, Japan, Netherlands, Norway, Singapore, Sweden, Switzerland, United Arab Emirates, United Kingdom, and the United States. Sixteen medium income countries included Croatia, Czech Republic, Greece, Hungary, Israel, Italy, Korea (South), Latvia, New Zealand, Poland, Portugal, Russia, Saudi Arabia, Slovenia, Spain, and Taiwan. Thirty eight low income countries included Algeria, Angola, Argentina, Bolivia, Bosnia and Herzegovina, Brazil, Chile, China, Columbia, Dominican Republic, Egypt, Ecuador, Guatemala, India, Indonesia, Iran, Jamaica, Jordan, Kazakhstan, Lebanon, Macedonia, Malaysia, Mexico, Morocco, Panama, Peru, Philippines, Romania, Serbia, South Africa, Syria, Thailand, Tonga, Tunisia, Turkey, Uganda, Uruguay, and Venezuela.

[10] SPSS Regression, Release 20.0, using stepwise procedure with the standard defaults.

in proportion to their percentage of all adults 18–64 years of age in the total sample of 74 countries. China and India have considerably more impact on the overall analysis than Iceland and Tonga.[11] As both independent and dependent variables represent the same time periods, any causal interpretations are to be considered speculative.

One adjustment in the daily income categories is made for these assessments. Only nine countries include individuals with very low levels of daily income, from $1.00 to $7.50. Reliable regression model development generally requires more than 9 units of analysis. These individuals, then, are combined with the next lowest category, $7.50 to $15.00 per day, to provide a sample of countries, 29, large enough for a useful regression analysis.

The resulting linear additive models for all countries and at each level of daily income are presented for nascent entrepreneurs in Table 7.1 and new firm owners in Table 7.2.

Table 7.1. Nascent entrepreneur national factor models: all and by daily income.

(Standardized beta coefficient in cells)	Overall	$60–$407/day	$30–$60/day	$15–$30/day	$1.00–$15/day
Number of countries	74	55	49	33	29
Percent variance explained (R*R)	72.0	84.9	76.1	75.9	70.2
Prevalence: nascent entrepreneurs/100 adults	4.8	4.2	4.6	5.6	7.2
Constant	0.03	0.34	0.38	0.20	0.38
Economic Characteristics					
High GDP per capita: $35–$57/K (2009: PPP) Yr:				N/A	N/A
Medium GDP per capita: $16–$35/K (2009: PPP) Yr:	*Base	Base	Base	Base	N/A
Low GDP per capita: $01–$16/K (2009: PPP) Yr:					
Per cent change GDP per capita: 2003–2008					
Annual pop growth: 1999–2009 (Avg)		−0.19		0.67	
Income inequality: 2000–2008 Average	0.28				

(*Continued*)

---

[11] These weights were re-centered for each of the five regression modeling exercises. The countries in each assessment group are listed by level of economic development in Appendix F.

Table 7.1.   (*Continued*)

(Standardized beta coefficient in cells)	Overall	$60–$407/day	$30–$60/day	$15–$30/day	$1.00–$15/day
Structural Features of the Economy					
Established firms/100 Persons 18–64 yrs old					
Percent agricultural workers: 2009					
Percent industrial workers: 2009	*Base	Base	Base	Base	Base
Percent service workers: 2009					
Centralized Control of Economic Activity					
Per cent government workers					
Gov spending as per cent of GDP					
Ease of business registration index	0.26				
Costs for commercial legal action Index					-0.58
Physical property rights recognition Index					
Intellectual property rights recognition Index					
Perceived corruption index: 2005					
Population Capacity for Business Creation					
National Index: Readiness for entrepreneurship	0.56		0.51	0.52	
Percent Total Population 25–44 yrs old					
Percent HS Degree or more 15+ years	0.27				
Percent women 15–64 yrs labor force: 2007				0.38	
Percent men 15–64 yrs labor force: 2007					
Unemployment rate: Avg 2000–2008					
National Cultural and Social Support					
Prevalence informal investors: #/100 Persons	0.45	0.67	0.55		0.73
National index of support for entrepreneurship					
Traditional (+1) vs. secular/rational (−1) values		0.65			1.14
Survival (+1) vs self-expressive (−1) values					

*Base: Not included in regression models to provide a base for comparison.
N/A: Not applicable, no cases in this cell for this analysis.

Table 7.2. New firm owner national factor models: all and by daily income.

	Overall	$60–$407/day	$30–$60/day	$15–$30/day	$1.00–$15/day
Number of countries	74	55	49	33	29
Percent variance explained (R*R)	92.8	80.4	88.1	93.2	96.8
Prevalence: new firm owners/100 adults	4.2	3.6	3.4	5.6	6.6
Constant	−1.20	−0.37	−0.08	−0.24	−1.88
Economic Characteristics					
High GDP per capita: $35–$57/K (2009: PPP) yr				N/A	N/A
Medium GDP per capita: $16–$35/K (2009: PPP) yr:	*Base	Base	Base	Base	N/A
Low GDP per capita: $01–$16/K (2009: PPP) yr:	0.29				
Percent change GDP per capita: 2003–2008	0.23	0.30	0.47		0.69
Annual pop growth: 1999–2009 (Avg)					
Income inequality: 2000–2008 average					
Structural Features of the Economy					
Established firms/100 persons 18–64 yrs old	0.61	0.59	0.43	0.71	0.84
Percent agricultural workers: 2009					−0.33
Percent industrial workers: 2009	*Base	Base	Base	Base	Base
Percent service workers: 2009					
Centralized Control of Economic Activity					
Percent government workers					
Gov spending as percent of GDP					
Ease of business registration index				0.18	
Costs for commercial legal action Index	−0.23				
Physical property rights recognition Index	−0.13				0.11
Intellectual property rights recognition Index					
Perceived corruption index: 2005				−0.16	
Population Capacity for Business Creation					
National index: readiness for entrepreneurship			0.24	0.18	
Percent total population 25–44 yrs old	0.19				0.48

(*Continued*)

Table 7.2.   (*Continued*)

	Overall	$60–$407/day	$30–$60/day	$15–$30/day	$1.00–$15/day
Percent HS Degree or more 15+ years	0.24				
Percent women 15–64 yrs Labor Force: 2007	0.44	0.26			0.68
Percent men 15–64 yrs labor force: 2007					
Unemployment rate: Avg 2000–2008					
National Cultural and Social Support					
Prevalence informal investors: #/100 persons	−0.12			−0.33	
National index: support for entrepreneurship				0.38	
Traditional (+1) vs. secular/rational (−1) values	−0.41	0.48			
Survival (+1) vs self-expressive (−1) values					

*Base: Not included in regression models to provide a base for comparison.
N/A: Not applicable, no cases in this cell for this analysis.

The top row indicates the number of countries in each assessment. As many countries with low average GDP per Capita have very high levels of income disparity, 20 of 38 low GDP per Capita countries are included in the high daily income regressions ($60 to $407, $30 to $60). In contrast, none of the high daily income countries are included in the regressions associated with the daily incomes below $30 per day.[12]

For models predicting the prevalence of nascent entrepreneurs at each daily income level, Table 7.1, the predictive success is relatively high. The overall model based on 74 countries accounts for 72% of the variation in the prevalence of nascent entrepreneurs with four national features. Predictive success for those at the four levels of daily income varies from 70% to 85%; results are best for the models involving a larger number of countries.

---

[12] The number of countries is less for the specific daily incomes; the actual countries are presented in Appendix F.

While there are differences among the models for nascent entrepreneurs associated with different levels of daily income, some national factors are presented in several models.

The prevalence of informal investors, those reporting they have recently provided funding to a new business that was not their own, is included in the overall and three daily income models. This would seem to be an indicator of the support one might expect from the local community for business creation; more informal investors are associated with more participation by nascent entrepreneurs.

The measure of readiness for entrepreneurship in the population is included in the overall model as well as two daily income models. As this index reflects the tendency among all adults to see business opportunities, know other entrepreneurs, and have confidence in their capacity to pursue business creation, it has a direct relationship to the measure of business creation. It is not included in models associated with the highest and lowest daily incomes. It is possible that this feature has a relatively uniform presence among countries included in these assessments and, hence, would not be associated with variation in prevalence of nascent entrepreneurs.

Another national factor that has a major impact in two models, $60–$407 per day and $1–$15 per day, is an emphasis on traditional rather than secular-rational values. The measures of national values are based on the data developed in the world values projects and reflect fundamental perspectives in different countries.[13] A traditional focus reflects an emphasis on work, a strong sense of responsibility for a family, an emphasis on self-reliance, and a reluctance to approach national agencies or government leaders for help with personal or family issues. An emphasis on secular-rational values, the opposite end of this dimension, would be associated with an assumption that collective solutions — government programs — are or should be established to assist with personal or family complications. Those with a traditional value emphasis are more likely to take individual actions to solve personal or household

---

[13] Inglehart (1990); Inglehart and Welzel (2005, 2010). The relevance to business creation is discussed in detail in Reynolds (2011, pp. 48–51).

problems, such as creating a new firm when suitable employment opportunities are not available.

The effects of other national factors are less systematic and do not provide a consistent image of associations related to differences in daily income levels. Lower costs for business registration appears to facilitate nascent entrepreneurs, but only those in the highest daily income group ($60–$407 per day). In contrast, higher commercial legal costs are associated with fewer nascent entrepreneurs in the second to the bottom income group ($7.50–$15 per day); perhaps this reflects a regulatory burden that discourages nascent entrepreneurs. A larger proportion of adults with high school degrees are associated with more nascent entrepreneurs in the overall model, a larger pool of educated adults may provide more involved in start-up efforts. More women involved in the labor force are associated with more nascent entrepreneurs in the $15–$30 per day model; this reflects a larger pool of candidates for nascent entrepreneurship.

The impact of recent population growth varies. In the highest daily income ($60–$407) model it has a negative association with nascent entrepreneurship, perhaps reflecting more competition from other young adults. In the model for those with daily incomes of $15–$30 a day, it has a positive association, perhaps reflecting an increase in demand that encourages more new firm creation.

A final observation is the lack of relationship to the levels of economic development, as reflected in annual GDP per Capita. It is included only in the overall model, this may reflect the positive relationship with income inequality, which is much higher for countries with lower annual GDP per capita, may be a more sensitive measure of lower levels of annual income.

The predictive success is slightly greater for the models related to the prevalence of new firm owners. As shown in Table 7.2, almost 93% of the variation in new firm owners is accounted for in the 74-country model, and from 80% to 97% in the models for different levels of daily income.

The one factor present in all models is the prevalence of established businesses. Based on the GEM surveys, this is a measure of the prevalence (number per 100 adults) of those that own businesses reporting profits for more than 42 months, referred to as established firms.[14] It provides a harmonized measure of the extent to which the national economy has a large number of established firms, most of which will be small. This may reflect an emphasis on sectors with low barriers to entry and more opportunities for workers to acquire small firm management experience, important for preparing individuals to create new firms. It is, therefore, reasonable to expect that countries with a larger proportion of economic activity in smaller firms will have higher prevalence rates of new firms.

The second most common factor is recent increases in GDP per Capita, which may reflect increases in demand. This would improve the customer base for new firms and enhance survival in their early years.

The other group of factors that appear to be important are the measure of the population readiness for entrepreneurship, the percentage of women active in the labor force, and the proportion of the total population 25–44 years old, an age when adults are quite active in business creation. This suggests that a national population of adults at the right stage in their life course and prepared to enter business creation is associated with more new firms.

Two measure of cultural and social support are incorporated in several models. An index of national support for entrepreneurship has a positive association in the $15–$30 per day model. The index of a national emphasis on traditional values has a positive association in the overall and highest daily income model. There is a small negative association with the prevalence of informal investors in the overall and $15–$30 per day models. Given the high association of the prevalence of informal investors and nascent entrepreneurs, this may reflect greater start-up activity and more competition for new firms, which may reduce the prevalence of new firms.

Four measures related to centralized control of economic activity have small and inconsistent impacts. Ease of business registration is

---

[14] In the earlier study (Reynolds, 2011) this measure included both new and established firms. It was revised for this analysis to avoid having the same measure included as both an independent and dependent variable.

associated with more new firms in the $15–$30 per day income categories. Higher costs for commercial legal action are associated with fewer new firms in the overall model. Greater perceived corruption is associated with fewer new firms in the $15–$30 per day income category. Greater recognition of physical property rights has an inconsistent association in two of the models. No broad generalizations about the impact of centralized control of economic activity are possible from this analysis.

Finally, there is an indication in the overall model that countries with low annual GDP per Capita will have more new firms. Among those with the lowest daily income ($1–$15 per day) there are fewer new firms where a higher proportion of workers are in agriculture.

This assessment has made clear that some national characteristics are systematically related to variation in the prevalence of participation in business creation.

- A general readiness for entrepreneurship and a presence of informal investors appears to be systematically associated with higher levels of participation by nascent entrepreneurs.
- A greater prevalence of existing (mostly small) firms, greater participation of women in the labor force and a recent increase in economic growth appears to be systematically associated with a greater prevalence of new firm owners.

There does not seem to be any major differences in national factors systematically related to different levels of daily income. The higher levels of business creation activity among those with lower level of daily income may be associated with differences in individual attributes, to be considered next.

7.2   National and Individual Factors and Business Creation: Multi-level Models

National factors are clearly associated with the amount of business creation activity in any given country. Individual participation in business creation is also affected by a number of personal attributes, such as gender, age, educational attainment, work force status, and, perhaps most significant, a readiness to pursue entrepreneurship. The research challenge is to assess the relative impact of these two types of factors, one reflecting the national context and the other individual attributes.

The same multi-level issues have emerged in many areas of social science, such as the education of students, performance in work groups and organizations, care in hospitals, outcomes of judicial proceedings, etc. In all cases there are both individual and contextual factors that appear to have significant impacts on the outcomes, such as academic achievement, work output and morale, personal health, or judicial decisions. Understanding the relative impact of national and personal factors affecting participation in firm creation is conceptually identical to these other phenomena.

This has led to the development of multi-level models. The basic strategy is to complete analysis at two levels. The initial level (level 1) utilizes regression analysis to develop linear additive models for each unique context. In this assessment these would be models using individual attributes to predict participation in new firm creation in each country. Each linear model is summarized by an intercept (a measured of the prevalence of activity in each country) and a slope (reflecting the success at using individual factors to predict individual activity). The result will be a range of results across the different countries. The next stage is to develop models that use national (level 2) features to predict, or explain, variation in the two characteristics of the level 1 linear models, the level of predicted activity (the intercept) and the impact of individual factors on the intercept (the slope).

The development and testing of the models involves a combination of standard regression procedures and multi-level analysis of variance (ANOVA). One of the most versatile procedures is the Hierarchical Linear Model Version 7 program (HLM7).[15] It will be used to explore the impact of national and individual factors on participation in business creation.

Hierarchical linear modeling procedures have several distinctive features. First, the assessments are based on applications using analysis

---

[15] Hofmann (1997), Hofmann and Gavin (1998), Raudenbush et al. (2011) and Snijders and Bosker (1999).

of variance (ANOVA), a procedure developed to assess differences in outcomes in controlled experiments. In these situations the investigator controls the impact on the participants in different conditions. When independent variables are controlled by the investigator there are no missing values. One of the distinctive characteristics of ANOVA procedures, then, is the requirement that there be no missing values on any variables used in the analysis. As a result, cases with any missing data must be eliminated from the file used for data analysis.

Second, the procedure is most efficient when the dependent measure is an interval level of measurement, such as relative mathematical aptitude, annual income, or years of survival following medical treatment. When the dependent variable is dichotomous, such as participating — or not — in a business startup, the assessment is less precise. Nevertheless, with a large enough sample of individuals and countries, the results can provide useful information. The actual implementation of model development with the HLM7 procedure is one of informed trial and error.[16]

As before, those identified as nascent entrepreneurs and new firm owners were the dependent variables or predicted outcomes. These are reflected as both individual attributes and as national prevalence rates.

Independent variables included both individual attributes (level 1) and national factors (level 2). The individual variables reflected gender, age, educational attainment, workforce status, household income relative to others in the country, and four measures of judgments about perception of opportunity, confidence in skills to pursue start-ups, knowing other entrepreneurs, and potential effects of fear of failure.[17] The national factors were those previously discussed and listed in the first column of Table 7.1.[18] Two types of weights are specified in these models. Level one or individual weights in each country are adjusted such that the national sample reflects the national adult population.

---

[16] For each specific model, predictor variables are entered based on informed judgments to identify that set that provide statistically significant, independent contributions to predicting the outcome while retaining about one level 2 (country) predictor for each ten level 2 units (countries) (Hoffman, 1997, p. 740). The procedures followed for developing these models are summarized in Appendix H.

[17] These variables and their coding are summarized in Appendix G.

[18] Sources are summarized in Appendix E.

Level two or country weights are those used in the previous assessment; each country is assigned a weight reflecting its proportion of the total population of adults in all the countries. Weights at both levels are adjusted to average 1.00.

The results of applying this procedure to predictions of the prevalence of nascent entrepreneurs and new firm owners for the total sample and for different levels of daily income are provided in Appendix I1 and I2.[19] Only those factors significant at least at the 0.05 level are included in the models; over four-fifths are significant beyond the 0.001 level. To present all statistically significant variables in a one-page chart, the national factors that were not statistically significant are omitted from the presentation. All were, however, initially considered as candidates in the early stages of model development. As all aspects of entrepreneurial readiness are included as individual attributes, the index reflecting entrepreneurial readiness was not among the national factors. Once again, as all data is to be considered cross-sectional in nature, causal interpretations must be made with some care.

The results of the MLM assessments are summarized in Table 7.3. The top half is related to the prevalence of nascent entrepreneurs and the bottom the prevalence of new firm owners. The success of the MLM models, based on predicting the national prevalence of participation in business creation, is comparable to that provided by the national characteristics models presented in Tables 7.1 and 7.2. Both sets of models are able to explain from 68% to 95% of the variation in national levels of business creation. This provides considerable confidence that major factors associated with business creation have been identified.

There are some differences in individual factors associated with nascent entrepreneurs at different levels of daily income. Men are more involved at most levels, but younger adults, those 18–24 years old, are more likely to be involved among those with lower daily incomes. A high school degree is associated with more activity at all daily income levels, and education beyond high school for the three higher levels of daily income. Among those with daily incomes from $1–$15 per day,

---

[19] Due to missing data on some individual characteristics, there is a slight reduction in the number of countries, from 74 to 72. The omitted countries (Yemen and West Bank/Gaza) were among those with the lowest GDP per capita.

Table 7.3.   Factors associated with business creation activity by daily income.

	Overall	$60–$407/Day	$30–$60/Day	$15–$30/Day	$1–$15/Day
*Nascent Entrepreneur**					
Nascent/100 adults	4.8	4.3	4.6	5.6	7.2
Variance explained	76.8%	82.8%	68.0%	70.6%	81.0%
Gender	Men	Men	Men	Men	Men
Age	18–24 yrs	25–34 yrs	25–44 yrs	18–24 yrs	18–34 yrs
Education	HS or more	HS or more	HS or more	HS or more	HS degree
Working	In labor force		In labor force	In labor force	
HH Income, relative		Lower	Middle	Middle	Upper
Entrepreneurial Readiness Items	Major positive	Major positive	Major positive	Major positive	Major positive
GDP/Capita: Low	Highest	High	Highest		
GDP/Capita: High	Higher		Higher		
Informal investors	Positive	Positive	Positive	Positive	Positive
Traditional values	Positive			Positive	Positive
New firm prevalence	Positive	Positive			
Percent agriculture workers	Negative	Negative			
*New Firm Owners***					
New Firm/100 adults	4.2	3.6	3.4	5.6	6.6
Variance explained	92.4%	77.9%	96.7%	97.1%	97.8%
Gender	Male	Male		Female	
Age	25–34 yrs	25–34 yrs	18–54 yrs	25–34 yrs	25–34 yrs
Education	Less grad exper	N/A	No HS degree	No HS Degree	N/A
Working	N/A	N/A	N/A	N/A	
HH Income, relative	Higher				Middle third
Entrepreneurial Readiness Items	Major positive	Major positive	Major positive	Major positive	Major positive
Fear of failure effect	Negative	Negative	Negative		Negative
GDP/Capita: Low					
GDP/Capita: High					
Growth GDP/Capita					
Nascent venture prevalence	Positive	Positive	Positive		Positive
Established firms prevalence	Positive	Positive	Positive	Positive	
Ease of business registration	Positive	Positive	Positive	Positive	Positive
Working women	Positive			Negative	
Informal investors	Negative			Positive	
National support					
Traditional values	Positive	Positive			Positive

education beyond high school is not associated with more participation as nascent entrepreneurs. Perhaps they have better prospects for income than starting a new firm.

Compared to those not in the labor force, individuals working full time or currently in the labor force seeking work are much more likely to be involved among those with intermediate levels of daily income, $30–$60 per day and $15–$30 per day, but there is no association among those at the highest and lowest levels of daily income.

While models are organized around those with different levels of daily income, there is additional information on each person's income relative to others in their country. They are classified as in the lowest third, middle third, or upper third in their national distributions. There is a dramatic patterns associated with different levels of daily income. Among those in the higher daily income categories, those with higher relative household income are less involved as nascent entrepreneurs. Among those in the lower daily income categories, those with higher relative household income are more involved. This suggests those in the higher daily income categories with higher household incomes have other more promising options. The reverse is true among those with lower daily income categories, where those from the highest household income categories may find firm creation their most promising option.

The most consistent and significant associations with participation as nascent entrepreneurs are related to aspects of personal readiness for entrepreneurship. In all models there are significant associations with the perception of business opportunities, confidence in start-up skills, and knowing other entrepreneurs.

National factors in these multi-level models related to nascent entrepreneurs are similar to those in the previous assessment, presented in the left column of Table 7.1. The major differences are greater uniformity across daily income models and fewer idiosyncratic national factors. The presence of informal investors is significant in all four models and an emphasis on traditional values is significant in three of the daily income models. Among those with the two highest daily incomes ($30–$60 and $60–$407 per day), those in the lowest GDP per Capita countries are more active as nascent entrepreneurs. Among those with daily income of \$30–\$60 per day, those in the highest GDP per capita countries are most active as nascent entrepreneurs. In the highest daily income model, those in countries with more emphasis on agriculture are slightly less likely to be involved as nascent entrepreneurs.

The multi-level models predicting the prevalence of new firm owners, summarized in Table 7.3, have considerable consistency across levels of daily income. Most striking is that women appear to be equally or more involved in three of the daily income models; men are more likely to be nascent entrepreneurs only in the high daily income model, \$60–\$407 per day. Women from higher income households are less likely to be involved. Associations of age with new firm owners are consistent across all daily income models; those 25 to 34 years of are more likely, and those over 54 years of age are less likely, to be new firm owners.

The association with education is quite distinctive, as there is no relationship among those with the highest and lowest daily income. But among those in the two intermediate daily income categories, \$30–\$60 per day and \$15–\$30 per day, those with more education are much less likely to be new firm owners. As the response of those that are new firm owners to questions about participation in the work force is somewhat ambiguous, it has been omitted from this analysis.

There is almost no association between the relative household income and participation as a new firm owner. It would appear that among those at the lowest daily income, \$1–\$15 per day, new firm owners are most likely to be in the middle third of their country's relative household income distribution.

The three facets of preparation for entrepreneurship are, once again, strongly associated with participation as a new firm owner. This is particularly true for confidence in skills to implement and manage a new firm.

Those that agree that "fear of failure" would discourage them from starting a new firm are more likely to be involved as a new firm owner. They have not, however, reported on whether or not they actually "fear failure."

National factors associated with participation as a new firm owner are also consistent. The prevalence of established firms, an indicator of a larger proportion of smaller firms, is positively associated with new firm ownership in all daily income models. Three factors — recent increase in GDP per Capita, more women in the labor force, and an emphasis on traditional values — are associated with more new firm owners in two models. A lower cost for business registration and greater national support for entrepreneurship is associated with more new firm ownership among those with daily incomes of \$15–\$30 per day. There is a small negative association with the prevalence of informal investors in this same daily income model. It may reflect more competition for new firms from investor sponsored nascent ventures.

Overall then, the multi-level modeling indicates small individual differences across those with different levels of daily income related to participation in new firm creation. Those active from groups with lower daily income tend to be somewhat younger, with less education, and from households with higher relative household income. At the country level more informal investors and an emphasis on traditional values appears to be associated with more nascent entrepreneurs. Those active as new firm owners are more likely to be women and perhaps from the middle third in terms of relative household income. Countries with a higher proportion of smaller firms, recent economic growth, and — for low daily income countries — more working women and an emphasis on traditional values appear to have more new firm owners.

The dominant factor associated with more nascent entrepreneurs and new firm owners across countries at all levels of daily income is personal readiness for entrepreneurship. All three factors — perceive opportunities, confidence in start-up skills, and knowing entrepreneurs — are associated with more business creation activity in almost all the daily income models. This justifies more attention to the diverse aspects of readiness for entrepreneurship.

7.3 Exploring Entrepreneurial Readiness

Both the national index of population readiness and the three specific aspects are major factors associated with business creation. An assessment of the factors affecting the three aspects of readiness for entrepreneurship will provide a more complete understanding of the intervening processes affecting business creation. These aspects include the perception of opportunities, confidence in the skill to implement a firm, and knowing others involved in business creation.

The strategy for this analysis is quite straightforward. The multi-level modeling assessment is repeated using the three components of the entrepreneurial readiness index as dependent variables. Except for the measures of entrepreneurial readiness at the national level, the same variables are candidates for inclusion as independent variables. The results, by daily income level, are presented in Appendix J1 for perception of good business opportunities, Appendix J2 for confidence in start-up skills, and Appendix J3 for personally knowing entrepreneurs. The major patterns are summarized in Table 7.4.

Across all countries and daily income levels the proportion that report they see good business opportunities is about 32%, that have confidence in their skills for starting a business is about 50%, and that know an entrepreneur is about 40%. The 15 multi-level models are reasonably successful; 13 explain 73% or more of the national variance; two models related to knowing an entrepreneur explain 48% and 63% of the variance.

The differences among the models related to the level of daily income are modest, compared to the differences among the three elements. Men are generally more likely to report yes to all three items, compared to women. The effect of age is different for the three items. Younger people are more likely to see opportunities and know an entrepreneur. For those with more than $30 in daily income, older persons are more likely to have confidence in their start-ups skills; for those with daily income below $30 it is the younger individuals.

The association of age, however, varies substantially for the three items. Those 25 to 54 years old are much more likely to report confidence in their start-up skills than those 18–24 or 55–64 years old. In contrast, perceptions of opportunities are greatest among those 18–24 years of age and knowing an entrepreneur is highest among those 18–34 years of age. The perception of opportunities or knowing an entrepreneur is less among older adults.

This represents a major conundrum, younger adults see opportunities and know others involved in business creation, yet older adults are more confident in their skills to successfully implement a business.

Table 7.4. Aspects of entrepreneurial readiness: daily income model overview.

	Perceive opportunities	Confidence in start-up skills	Know an entrepreneur
Percent yes (range)	28–42%	45–58%	35–44%
Explained variance	76–82%	79–95%	48–87%
Personal Characteristics			
Gender	Men generally Below $15 DI: Women	Men: All DI levels	Men: All DI levels
Age:	Younger generally	Above $30 DI: Older	Above $15 DI: Younger
	Little effect: $30–$60 DI	Below $30 DI: Younger	Below $15 DI: No effect
Educational Attainment	More education	More education	More education
Labor force status	Working: All levels	Working: All levels	Working: All levels
Relative HH Income	Above $30 DI: Higher	Above $30 DI: Higher levels	Above $30 DI: Higher levels
	Below $30 DI: No effect	Below $15 DI: Lower levels	Below $30 DI: No effect
National Factors			
National GDP per Capita	Above $30 DI: Lower income	Above $30 DI: Lower income	$30-60 DI: Lower income
	Below $30 DI: No effect	Below $30 DI: No effect	
Growth GDP per Capita	Small effect: 2 DI levels	Small effect: 2 DI levels	Small effect: 1 DI level
Growth: Human population	Major effect: all DI levels	Major effect: 2 DI levels	Major effect: 3 DI levels
Traditional values	Major effect: 2 DI levels	Major effect: 3 DI levels	Reverse effect: 1 DI level
Self-expressive values	Major effect: 2 DI levels	Major effect: 2 DI levels	Reverse effect: 1 DI level
Source	Appendix J1	Appendix J2	Appendix J3

There may be an optimum age, perhaps in the early 30s, where a person is young enough to see opportunities and have a supportive social network of other entrepreneurs but old enough to have developed useful skills and experience.

Educational attainment and, with a strong relationship, working full or part time are generally associated with all three aspects for those at all income levels.

The association with relative household income, compared to others in the same country, varies for the level of daily income. Among those with $30 a day or more in income, those with higher relative household income are more likely to see opportunities, have confidence in their start-up skills, and know an entrepreneur. For those with daily income below $30, there is little systematic impact, although among those with daily income below $15 with less relative household income have more confidence in their start-up skills.

Among the national factors there is an interaction between the national level of development, represented by annual GDP per capita, and the level of daily income. Those with daily income above $30 in less developed countries are more likely to see opportunities and have confidence in their skills to start a business. Those with daily income from $30 to $60 in developing countries are more likely to know an entrepreneur. Few high income countries have individuals at very low levels of daily income, preventing assessment of this relationship.

Countries with recent increases in GDP per Capita and recent growth in the adult population — two factors that would increase demand for goods and services — are associated with a more positive response to all three items. Those in countries with the lowest per capita income are more likely to perceive business opportunities. Those in countries with a higher prevalence of established firms, those economies with more small firms, are likely to have a greater prevalence of start-up skills and knowledge of other entrepreneurs.

Two national values have a significant association with the perception of opportunity and confidence in start-up skills. In those countries emphasizing traditional values (with a major focus on self-reliance) and self-expression values the residents are more likely to see good business opportunities and have confidence in their start-up skills. The association with knowing other entrepreneurs is more modest, present in only one model for each, and the models are different for each value.

The joint global distribution of these national values for the World Value Survey countries is presented in Figure 6.3. This indicates that most countries are clustered in groups that share a common history and political development, reflected in similar emphases on these two value dimensions.

Many of the developing countries, the context for those with low levels of daily income, are in the bottom or left sections of Figure 6.3.

Many countries of Africa and Asia, particularly those with an Islamic tradition, with low GDP per Capita tend to be in the lower left quadrant, strong on traditional values but with an emphasis on survival rather than self-expressive values. Latin American countries appear to be strong on tradition and intermediate on survival versus self-expressive values. European countries tend to be in the upper right quadrant, high on both secular-rational and self-expressive values.

A unique group of countries have a strong national emphasis on self-expression and an intermediate emphasis on the traditional versus

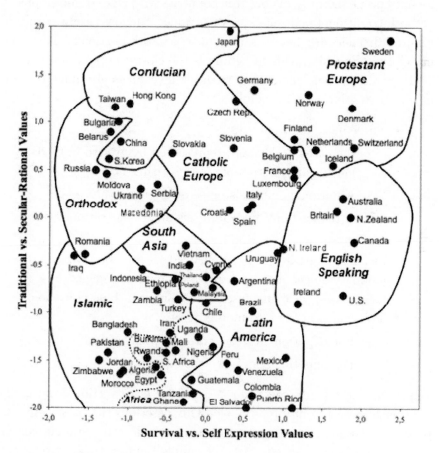

Fig. 7.3 National value dimensions and country groups.[20]

---

[20] Inglehart and Welzel (2010).

secular-rational dimension. As seen in Figure 7.3, this appears to include seven "English Speaking" countries, of which four are not in Europe (Australia, Canada, New Zealand, and the United States). These North American, Oceanic countries have a level of business creation that is about twice that of other high income countries, including "English Speaking" European countries.[21] If there is a "positive entrepreneurial climate," it may be a reflection of this unique combination of these two fundamental national values.

Based on the previous assessment, the strongest impact on readiness for entrepreneurship would occur in countries with an extreme emphasis on both traditional and self-expressive values, the lower right corner of Figure 7.3. There are, however, no countries in this portion of the "value map," the "English Speaking" group is the closest approximation.

It would appear, then, that a major mechanism leading to more new firm creation may be as follows:

- Three national attributes:
  - Increases in demand, represented by growth in GDP per Capita and population growth,
  - A national emphasis on self-expressive values, and
  - A reduced national emphasis on secular-rational values.
- Leads to greater entrepreneurial readiness, particularly among younger men with more education, engaged in work for pay and, in many cases, from higher income households.
- This leads, in turn, to more:
  - Participation as a nascent entrepreneur and
  - Participation as a new firm owner.

While this causal interpretation is based on cross-sectional data, the relationships seem quite reasonable. This describes the most common path to entrepreneurship, and does not exclude other individuals or factors from having an effect. For example, among those with lower daily income women are as likely to be involved as men.

---

[21] Reynolds (2011, Figure 6.1, p. 74).

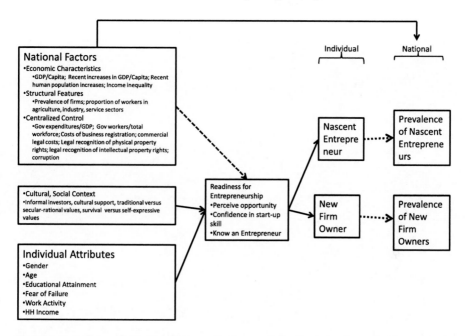

Fig. 7.4 National and individual factors affecting participation in business creation, revised.

But the major intervening factor between national characteristics and the presence of new firms is the action of individuals, those that create the new firms. A revision of the model presented in Figure 7.1 as Figure 7.4 helps clarify this relationship.

This model places individual readiness for entrepreneurship at the center of the causal process and gives special emphasis to the social and cultural context, reflected in the informal institutions. It suggests that a major challenge for policy makers may be affecting well established national values, the values that are a major factor affecting how individuals respond to work and career options.

8

Overview and Implications

Billions of world citizens, the poor, are in situations with limited options for developing useful work. The major focus of this assessment has been to explore the amount and nature of their participation in business creation. Harmonized data collected from representative samples of the adult population in 74 countries over the 2000 to 2009 period was used to estimate the number of individuals active in firm creation with different levels of daily income. Almost half, 48%, of the 4.2 billion midlife adults are in the two lowest economic status levels, with daily household incomes of less than $15 per day. Within this group of 1.8 billion, over 40% are 18–34 years old, two-thirds have not completed high school, and gender is evenly balanced.

Yet among the 211 million involved in start-ups and 236 million new firm owners about half, 97 million nascent entrepreneurs and 113 million owner managers, are from the 1.8 billion at the bottom. Most from the bottom billions are in developing Asian countries, although they are well represented in Sub-Sahara Africa, the Middle East and North Africa, and Latin America. Women make up about 40% of those involved in business creation, with a slightly higher proportion from groups with less daily income. Those involved in business creation from the bottom billions are much less likely to have completed high school. They are generally from the poorest households in their countries, truly at the bottom, and are less likely to be prepared for entrepreneurship.

Those from the bottom billion are more likely to be involved in business creation if they are male, younger, working, see business opportunities, know other entrepreneurs, and are confident in their skills in business creation. A positive judgement about the climate for entrepreneurship also helps.

The 46 million nascent ventures and 80 million new firms implemented by the those with daily household incomes of less than $15 are operating in all economic sectors, and a substantial minority plan to create more than 20 jobs, are in high technology sectors, expect to have an impact on the markets in which they compete, and expect to service customers outside their countries. In summary, the firms implemented by the bottom billion are not only providing useful work for their owners, but are an important share of high potential firms.

Further, the bottom billions are involved in about half of all new firm creation which, in turn, is responsible for a third of all new job creation. These individuals are providing replacement jobs to compensate for the high levels of job termination found in economies undergoing major structural change as well as substantial growth.

The same national factors tended to be associated with differences in business creation activity for those with different levels of daily income. At all levels of daily income, countries with more citizens ready for entrepreneurship and with a greater presence of informal investors appear to have more nascent entrepreneurs. Countries with more existing firms, more women in the labor force, and a reduced proportion of workers in agricultural sectors have more new firm owners.

As one might expect, virtually all of this bottom billion business creation is occuring where the bottom billion live, in developing, or low income countries in Asia, Sub-Sahara Africa, Latin America and the Middle East North African regions.

Although a large proportion of the bottom billion are engaged out of necessity, many are able to develop profitable enterprises; once they are managing profitable new firms they find this a better option than work for pay. There is not, at this time, reliable longitudinal data on the success of transforming nascent ventures into profitable new firms among the bottom billions, although such studies have been completed in a number of advanced counries.[1]

8.1 Understanding Business Creation

This assessment has implications for understanding business creation related to the conception of institutional factors affecting economic behavior; variations in the processes across those with different levels of daily income and, in turn, different levels of national economic development; the capacity for explaining high levels of national variation; and understanding the business creation process.

First, the assessment is consistent with a focus on formal and informal institutions as major factors affecting economic activity and economic growth. There is strong evidence that the informal institutions, the established culture and value systems in a country, have considerable influence over whether or not individuals pursue business creation. This is reflected in the association of an emphasis on traditional and self-expressive values on personal readiness for entrepreneurship. These informal institutions seem to have much more influence than formal institutions on individual participation in business creation.

Second, the assessments have several unique features. Perhaps most fundamental is portraying business creation among the global population of over 3 billion midlife adults, representing 80% of the global population of midlife adults. Some of the patterns are quite different from those found in developed countries, where the vast majority of entrepreneurial research has been completed. For example, in low national income countries, the very youngest adults (those 18–24 years old) were most active as nascent entrepreneurs compared to high national income countries, where those 25–34 years old were the most active. Further, while men are more active in higher national income countries, there is gender equality of participation among nascent entrepreneurs in low national income countries and there are more women among new firm owners.

---

[1] This includes Australia, Canada, Germany, Latvia, Netherlands, Norway, Sweden and the United States and urban areas in China (Reynolds and Curtin, 2011).

There was a complete reversal of association related to relative household income. Among those with higher daily incomes, there was less business creation among those with higher relative household incomes. Among those with lower daily incomes, business creation was more prevalent among those with high relative household incomes. This suggests that considerable caution is required in extrapolating results from developed countries (where high daily incomes are found) to the emerging countries (where most low daily incomes are located).

Third, the relatively high levels of explained variance, representing a predictive success, across a range of assessments suggests that many of the most significant factors, individual and national, have been identified. Other analyses may locate other features that are important, but these new predictors will probably be correlated with the variables included in this assessment.

Fourth, the assessment has identified a major individual characteristic that is central to this process. Those that consider themselves ready for entrepreneurship are much more likely to take action. In addition, several national factors with a major impact on readiness for entrepreneurship have been identified, specifically growth in demand as well as national values that encourage self-reliance (traditional rather than secular-rational values) and individual self-expression.

On the other hand, there is much more to be learned about business creation; this analysis is only one step forward.

8.2   Next Steps

The value of using multiple assessments to develop an understanding of factors affecting the firm creation process has been illustrated. The linear additive models based on national attributes using standardized regression and multi-level modeling procedures had complementary results. This increases confidence that the major national and individual factors associated with business creation have been identified.

Strong confidence in causal relationships are hampered by the cross-sectional nature of the analysis. This reflects several complications. The first is the lack of annual data on business creation for a number of countries, particularly developing countries with modest resources to implement GEM adult population surveys on an annual basis. In order to minimize country level measurement errors, national samples were consolidated across years. On the other hand, except for rare and dramatic "economic shocks," year to year changes within a country are small, compared to the massive differences across countries. Second, and equally important, is the lack of temporal precision on many national factors, which were developed from aggregating measures across multiple years, usually from 2000 to 2009. Until more precise annual data is available on independent and dependent variables, strong confidence in causal inferences will not be possible.

Over half of the samples represent advanced countries where there were the resources to complete annual adult population surveys following the GEM protocol. This was compensated for, in part, by using case and national weights to increase the impact of smaller samples from the developing countries. But these smaller samples can lead to more measurement error for those cases representing the largest portion of the population. More data collection in developing countries, particularly Sub-Sahara Africa, would provide an improved global assessment. This would be unlikely, however, to have a significant impact on the major results.

A final complication is the static analysis of the firm creation process. The comparisons of different stages are based on assessments of different nascent entrepreneurs and new firms at the same point in time. Until longitudinal studies of representative cohorts are completed, the understanding of how individuals and teams progress from start-ups to new firms to established firms will be incomplete. Given the evidence that firm creation may take a different form in countries at different levels of development, longitudinal studies have great potential for improving understanding of the process. Such studies have been implemented in a number of advanced countries and urban areas in China; they provide a useful template for expansion to the developing world.[2]

_____

[2] Reynolds and Curtin (2010).

8.3   Policy Implications

Perhaps the most important policy implication is that a very substantial number of those with low levels of daily income are involved in business creation where they live. These tens of millions far outweigh the minority, in the hundreds of thousands, that emigrate to find more rewarding work, or the few, in the thousands, that puruse illegal pursuits or engage in terrorism. Most people with low levels of income attempt to survive following a traditional route. They make an effort to develop an economic speciality that can provide a valued product or service to others. If even one-third of the 96 million nascent entrepreneurs from the bottom billion are able to develop a profitable situation for self-employment, it would provide over half, 30 million, of the 53 million job shortfall that has been projected for developing countries. The evidence that half of new firms and one-third of new firm jobs are created by those with daily household incomes below $15 suggests they make a substantial contribution to replacing jobs lost from firm contraction and discontinuation.

The second implication is related to the major disadvantage for the bottom billion — a lack of a general education. Most have not completed a secondary (high) school program. It is difficult to implement and manage any business venture without the capacity to read, write, and do arthimetic. This is related to one of the major factors that separates the poor, and the not so poor as well, that pursue business creation from those that do not — confidence in the personal capacity to manage a business. This provides a strong recommendation for providing an education to all segments in all countries. More training and experience in business matters, either in school or on the job, would also be an asset.

A third implication is related to finance. Harmonized measures of the availability, or actual access to formal financial support were not available. A harmonized measure of early financial support for all countries in the analysis was the prevalence of informal investors. This was universally associated with more nascent entrepreneurs. This suggests that the availability of early financial support, often very modest amounts, may help many start-ups in their initial stages. The emphasis on microfinance may be well placed. On the other hand, the demand is enormous, involving tens of millions of nascent ventures and new firms.

A fourth implication is that governments might develop more support for those that are attempting to overcome their economic plight through firm creation. Many accustomed to the formal, well regulated world of advanced countries have emphasized the low productivity, poor working conditions, and the avoidance of taxes and regulations associated with the informal (unregistered) economy, the firms implemented by the bottom billions.[3] Such commentaries do not reflect concern for the alternatives confronting those attempting to participate in the economy to support their families. The implementation of complex, expensive, and onerous registration and licensing requirements — which may be ignored by those desperate to care for themselves and their families — are probably not a good strategy for encouraging firm creation and national economic growth.

As reflected in the opening quote, "The poor also have the right to buy and sell!" the clumsy and heavy-handed implementation of regulations were clearly a major factor in the 2011 Arab uprisings. If firm registration was associated with positive benefits for the owners, such as access to microfinance and financial institutions, legitimate standing in the legal system, and participation in assistance, retirement, and health care programs, rather than only a first step in the payment of required taxes, it would benefit all concerned.

Whatever the success and contributions of the new ventures launched by the bottom billions, they provide the start-up teams with a more useful choice than high risk economic migration, criminal enterprises, terrorism or violent revolutions. Systematic assistance for the millions from the bottom billions involved in firm creation would have substantial benefits.

---

[3] de Paula and Scheinkman (2007).

A

GEM Data Processing

The assessment is based on annual data collection completed in the Global Entrepreneurship Monitor [GEM] program initiated in 1998. From 2000 to 2009 almost 400 annual national surveys were completed in 77 countries resulting in 1,250,303 interviews. However, once those under 18 or over 65 and the 20% where data on annual income is missing are eliminated, the data set is reduced to 836,956 interviews completed in 74 countries. As each country is represented by a national team and each team must raise the funds to complete their own data collection, not all countries were involved in each year. Each survey involved locating a representative sample of the adult population which was provided with a standard set of questions about participation in different stages of the firm life course, from creation through management of new and established firms. While the interview schedules were translated and administered in the appropriate language of each country, the resulting data sets were translated into English for consolidated analysis and overview reports completed each year. The analysis procedure was as follows:

(1) Data sets, reflecting the responses to the basic items, for each year were assembled and harmonized to ensure that coding of

all responses was uniform across the 10 years (2000 through 2009); this compensated for variation in some interview procedures as items and response categories were "adjusted."

(2) Initial case weights were checked to ensure they provided a representation of the adult population in each country.

(3) All transforms and indices, including identifying those at different stages of the firm life course, were completed on the full consolidated, harmonized data set of 1.2 million cases.

(4) The size of the adult population, 18–64 years in age, was determined for all 74 countries as of 2009. The number of respondents in each country, 18–64 years in age, was available from the samples in the data set. Case weights were adjusted to reflect the proportion of the adults in the total population represented by each country. Hence, cases in smaller countries with large sample populations, such as Spain, had much smaller case weights than cases from very large countries with small sample populations, such as China and India.

(5) Estimates of the prevalence rates for different types of business creation activity were developed for each of the eight global regions.

(6) These prevalence rates where multiplied by the number of adults, 18–64 years old, in each global region to create estimates of the number of individuals in the total population for each region.

While this procedure is subject to sampling and estimation errors, it does provide a reasonable first approximation on the level of business creation and business ownership for these countries and regions.

B

Estimating Annual Income

All interviews completed as part of the GEM surveys involved items related to household personal income. As the data was collected by a diverse group of commercial survey firms, there was considerable variation in the procedures and nature of the response alternatives. To provide some measure of standardization across countries, respondent annual income data was converted into one of three categories — lowest third, middle third, and upper third — of the distribution in each national sample. While this provide within country comparisons, it does not allow for cross national comparisons.

The following procedure was employed to facilitate cross-national comparisons. It began with the United National University — World Institute for Development Economics Research data base on Income Inequality (accessed 2 Jan 2012). While this data base provides harmonized measures of the Gini coefficient reflecting income inequality, it also includes estimates of the proportion of total national income (or consumption) associated with each rank ordered quintiles (five categories) or deciles (10 categories) of the population. Maximum equality would occur when each quintile received exactly 20% of the total income (or was responsible for 20% of the total consumption) or each decile received exactly 10% of the total income (or was responsible for 10% of the total consumption). This information was used to assign the values to the GEM respondents in each third of the relative national income distribution.

The procedure is illustrated for Venezuela, where data on the distribution of income by decile was available for 2005, presented in Table B.1

The first column reflects the percentage of the population in each category, deciles and thirds. The second column is the data provided by the UNU-WIDER data base for 2005, showing the proportion of total national income associated with each decile of population. The third column shows the decile data from column two converted to thirds. The fourth column presents the ratio of the highest and lowest thirds to the middle third. The fifth column shows the annual GDP per capita in US dollars adjusted for purchasing power parity; the middle third value is the national average for 2009 from the WEO database. The highest and lowest third were calculated based on the ratios in the fourth column. The final column shows the daily GDP per Capita, based on the annual GDP per Capita divided by 365.

The result of the procedure is reflected in the Table B.2. Countries are rank ordered by their GDP per Capita for 2009 provided in the

Table B.1.   Estimates for Venezuela.

Population percentile (%)	Proportion of income: deciles (%)	Proportion of income: thirds (%)	Ratio to middle third	Annual GDP per Capita: 2009 US$ (PPP)	Daily GDP per Capita: 2009 US$ (PPP)
68–100		66.8	2.77	US$ 38,280	US$ 100.88
91–100	35.7				
81–90	16.2				
71–80	12.0				
34–67		24.1	1.00	US$ 13,293	US$ 36.82
61–70	9.55				
51–60	7.7				
41–50	6.3				
31–40	5.0				
00–33		9.1	0.38	US$ 5,000	US$ 13.70
21–30	3.9				
11–20	2.7				
0–10	1.0				
All	100.0	100.0			

Table B.2.

Country	Latest GINI year	GINI value	GDP/PC (PPP): 2009	Ratio: bottom /middle	Ratio top /middle	Bottom Third: daily income	Middle Third: Daily income	Top Third: daily income
Norway	2002	37.0	57,434	0.44	2.03	68.76	157.35	320.06
Singapore	1980	39.5	54,194	0.54	2.45	79.92	148.48	363.25
United States	2004	46.4	47,178	0.35	2.52	45.25	129.25	325.72
Hong Kong	1996	51.4	46,832	0.40	3.18	50.92	128.31	407.45
Ireland	2001	28.9	46,148	0.51	1.66	64.42	126.43	209.25
Switzerland	1992	35.9	43,565	0.48	2.03	57.64	119.36	242.55
Austria	2001	23.7	41,178	0.60	1.53	67.76	112.82	172.19
Netherlands	2001	25.8	41,042	0.64	1.66	71.99	112.44	186.66
Canada	2000	32.4	40,125	0.52	1.89	56.76	109.93	207.46
Iceland	MISS	MISS	39,668	0.53	1.89	57.52	108.68	205.29
United Arab Emirates	MISS	MISS	39,262	0.50	2.20	53.98	107.57	236.87
Denmark	2002	39.0	39,252	0.43	2.21	45.93	107.54	237.34
Australia	2004	29.3	39,067	0.55	1.71	58.39	107.03	183.55
Sweden	2003	25.2	38,924	0.63	1.66	67.28	106.64	176.87
Finland	2003	25.6	38,144	0.62	1.66	65.03	104.50	173.10
United Kingdom	2002	34.2	37,494	0.54	2.03	55.50	102.72	208.02
Belgium	2001	29.3	37,043	0.59	1.83	60.05	101.49	186.12
Germany	2004	31.1	36,447	0.53	1.85	53.34	99.85	184.54
Japan	1993	24.8	35,924	0.66	1.65	64.48	98.42	162.57
France	2001	27.6	35,008	0.59	1.71	56.73	95.91	163.93
Taiwan	2003	33.9	33,096	0.50	1.91	45.60	90.67	172.74
Greece	2001	32.3	32,273	0.51	1.90	45.11	88.42	168.18
Italy	2002	35.9	31,555	0.47	2.05	41.03	86.45	177.36
Spain	2005	33.4	31,374	0.52	1.96	44.72	85.96	168.05
Slovenia	2001	24.5	30,350	0.62	1.60	51.16	83.15	133.05
New Zealand	1996	40.2	27,952	0.46	2.35	34.99	76.58	180.01
Korea, Republic of	1998	37.2	27,863	0.38	1.94	29.27	76.34	148.29
Czech Republic	2003	22.8	27,443	0.64	1.57	47.95	75.19	117.73
Israel	2001	38.9	27,323	0.45	2.22	33.56	74.86	166.39
Saudi Arabia	MISS	MISS	25,428	0.50	2.20	34.96	69.67	153.41
Portugal	2001	37.1	23,024	0.53	2.25	33.22	63.08	142.05
Hungary	2003	25.2	20,705	0.61	1.62	34.39	56.73	91.93
Latvia	2003	35.9	18,983	0.55	2.19	28.83	52.01	113.99
Poland	2003	35.2	18,640	0.49	2.02	24.95	51.07	103.09
Puerto Rico	2003	52.9	18,300	0.32	3.11	15.94	50.14	155.97
Croatia	2005	29.0	17,507	0.58	1.76	27.95	47.96	84.52
Russian Federation	2002	31.0	17,494	0.56	1.85	26.78	47.93	88.51
Chile	2003	54.6	15,424	0.43	3.73	18.11	42.26	157.77
Argentina	2006	48.3	15,147	0.37	2.87	15.22	41.50	119.08

(*Continued*)

Table B.2.   (*Continued*)

Country	Latest GINI year	GINI value	GDP/PC (PPP): 2009	Ratio: bottom /middle	Ratio top /middle	Bottom Third: daily income	Middle Third: daily income	Top Third: Daily income
Malaysia	1995	50.0	14,776	0.42	3.20	16.94	40.48	129.39
Turkey	2000	40.0	14,184	0.50	2.32	19.24	38.86	90.15
Mexico	2005	51.0	13,532	0.40	3.20	14.87	37.07	118.51
Uruguay	2005	45.0	13,305	0.42	2.68	15.36	36.45	97.81
Venezuela	2005	47.6	13,293	0.38	2.77	13.70	36.42	100.88
Romania	2002	32.7	13,146	0.55	1.94	19.96	36.02	69.93
Kazakhstan	MISS	MISS	12,910	0.48	2.26	17.08	35.37	79.99
Lebanon	1960	60.4	12,277	0.25	3.12	8.43	33.64	105.01
Panama	2004	54.8	11,943	0.33	3.59	10.73	32.72	117.34
Serbia and Montenegro	2001	28.1	11,819	0.60	1.76	19.28	32.38	56.94
Iran	2005	38.4	11,752	0.50	2.20	16.16	32.20	70.90
South Africa	2000	56.5	10,718	0.41	3.98	11.99	29.37	116.96
Brazil	2005	56.4	10,649	0.36	3.85	10.52	29.18	112.20
Macedonia, FYR	2003	35.2	9,592	0.34	1.75	8.89	26.28	45.97
Thailand	2002	42.0	8,942	0.52	2.53	12.67	24.50	62.01
Peru	2005	47.7	8,909	0.41	2.94	10.02	24.41	71.66
Tunisia	2000	40.6	8,451	0.49	2.36	11.30	23.15	54.68
Jamaica	2004	45.5	8,334	0.48	2.75	10.87	22.83	62.74
Bosnia and Herzegovina	2005	35.8	7,922	0.52	2.07	11.34	21.70	45.03
Ecuador	2006	53.4	7,786	0.40	3.48	8.59	21.33	74.21
Dominican Republic	2006	51.9	7,693	0.41	3.36	8.71	21.08	70.91
Colombia	2004	56.2	7,393	0.36	3.81	7.38	20.25	77.11
Algeria	1995	35.4	7,247	0.51	2.08	10.04	19.85	41.36
Angola	MISS	MISS	7,188	0.36	5.15	7.18	19.69	101.49
China	2002	45.4	6,509	0.40	2.76	7.21	17.83	49.28
Egypt	2004	34.4	6,279	0.62	1.98	10.66	17.20	34.13
Jordan	2003	38.8	5,413	0.52	2.30	7.77	14.83	34.05
Tonga	MISS	MISS	5,412	0.47	2.88	6.97	14.83	42.64
Guatemala	2004	49.4	5,087	0.39	3.02	5.44	13.94	42.12
Syria	MISS	MISS	4,839	0.56	2.17	7.47	13.26	28.71
Morocco	1999	39.4	4,587	0.52	2.33	6.48	12.57	29.26
Bolivia	2004	50.5	4,403	0.46	3.32	5.56	12.06	40.05
Indonesia	2005	39.4	4,251	0.56	2.39	6.51	11.65	27.88
Philippines	2003	47.9	3,776	0.43	3.04	4.49	10.34	31.42
India	2004	36.8	3,129	0.59	2.25	5.08	8.57	19.30
West Bank/Gaza	MISS	MISS	2,900	0.25	3.12	1.99	7.95	24.80
Yemen, Republic of	2005	37.7	2,569	0.55	2.22	3.86	7.04	15.60
Uganda	2002	45.7	1,041	0.51	2.80	1.45	2.85	7.98

fourth column. The following steps were involved:

(1) For each country included in the UNU-WIDER data set, the data on the most recent year that covered all of the adult population in all geographic regions was identified. If there was a choice, decile data was chosen over quintile data and data associated with a higher Gini coefficients was chosen. This data was available for 69 countries in the GEM data set, with data for 59 from the year 2000 to 2006, for 8 from 1992 to 1999, and for two prior to 1992. In the Table B.2, those without data are indicated by "miss" in the second and third columns.

(2) This information was then used to estimate the income (or consumption) distribution in three ranked categories, lowest third, middle third, and highest third.

(3) The ratio of the lowest third to the middle third and the highest third to the middle third was computed for each GEM country, presented in columns 5 and 6 of the Table B.2.

(4) Data for GEM countries not represented in the UNU-WIDER data set was estimated as follows:

   a. Iceland was set to the average of Nordic countries: Denmark, Finland, Norway and Sweden.

   b. Angola was set to the average of adjacent countries with data: Botswana, Namibia, and Zambia.

   c. Kazakhstan was set to the average of adjacent countries with data: Kyrgyz Republic, Tajikistan, Turkmenistan, and Uzbekistan.

   d. Syria was set to the average of Egypt, Jordan, and Yemen.

   e. West Bank/Gaza was set to the values of Lebanon.

   f. Saudi Arabia and United Arab Emirates were set the values of Iran.

   g. Tonga was set to the average of Malaysia, Indonesia, and Philippines.

(5) Those in the middle third were assigned annual GDP per Capita from the IMF World Economic Outlook in US$ adjusted for purchasing power parity for 2009.

(6) Those in the upper third or lower third were assigned annual GDP per capita consistent with the ratios computed from the measures of income distribution.

(7) Daily income was computed by dividing annual income by 365.

(8) Individuals in the GEM data set in the lowest, middle and upper third of their national income distributions were assigned the values in the three right hand columns of the Table B.2.

While there is no question this procedure is subject to considerable errors at many stages, it does provide an approximate daily income estimate that is standardized across all countries and takes differences in purchasing power parity (standard of living) into account.

C

Global Regions

Eight global regions are used in this assessment. The countries in each region from the GEM data set are provided in Table C.1. As they share a common heritage and have very similar business creation profiles, the four non-European Anglo countries — Australia, Canada, New Zealand, and the United States are treated as a single "region" referred to as North America, Oceania. Other assessments have referred to these countries as "Western Offshoots" (Milanovic, 2011, p. 143). The other seven regions are generally composed of contiguous countries. As there is very little difference in business creation profiles of low and high income countries in the Central, Eastern European and in the MENA region (Reynolds, 2011), they are combined for this analysis. In contrast, there are dramatic differences between the low and high income Asian countries so they are separated for this assessment.

A comparison of the countries in the GEM sample with a global count of countries, based on the latest International Finance Corporation World Economic Outlook population estimates, is provided in Table C.2. Of the 184 countries in the IFC WEO database, representative surveys providing the necessary data have been completed in 74 as part of the GEM initiative. More significant, of the estimated world

Table C.1. GEM sample countries by world region classification.

	GDP/Capita less than US$ 20,000/year	GDP/Capita greater than US$ 20,000/year
North America, Oceania		Australia, Canada, New Zealand, United States
Western Europe, Israel		Austria, Belgium, Denmark, Finland, France, Germany, Greece, Iceland, Israel, Ireland, Italy, Netherlands, Norway, Portugal, Spain, Sweden, Switzerland, United Kingdom
Central, Eastern Europe	Czech Republic, Croatia, Kazakhstan, Macedonia, Poland, Romania, Russia, Serbia	Czech Republic, Hungary, Slovenia
Asia: Developed		Hong Kong, Japan, Korea (South), Singapore
Asia: Developing	China, India, Indonesia, Malaysia, Philippines, Thailand, Tobago	
Middle East, North Africa	Algeria, Egypt, Iran, Jordan, Lebanon, Morocco, Syria, Tunisia, Turkey, Palestine (West Bank/Gaza), Yemen	Saudi Arabia, United Arab Emirates
Latin America, Caribbean	Argentina, Bolivia, Brazil, Chile, Columbia, Dominican Republic, Ecuador, Guatemala, Jamaica, Mexico, Panama, Peru, Uruguay, Venezuela	
Sub-Sahara Africa	South Africa, Uganda	

population of 6,726 million in 2009, 5,142 million, or 76.4%, are covered by the GEM countries.

Table C.2 makes clear that the GEM surveys cover over 90% of the population in four regions, over 80% of the population in six regions, and over 50% in seven regions. There is, however, a major shortfall in Sub-Sahara Africa. In this region GEM surveys have been completed in 2 of 44 countries representing slightly more than 10% of the total population. As a result, it should be no surprise if some estimates for Sub-Sahara Africa seem "unusual."

Table C.2.   GEM sample countries compared with global counts.

Global region	WEO count	GEM count	WEO 2010 population (Millions)	GEM 2009 population (Millions)	GEM/WEO proportion (%)	Total 2010 population: 18–64 yrs old (Millions)
North America, Oceania	4	4	371	366	98.6	233
Western Europe, Israel	21	18	418	407	97.4	263
Central, Eastern Europe	30	12	477	259	54.3	320
Asia: Developed	5	4	212	187	88.2	135
Asia: Developing	28	7	3,555	2,926	82.3	2,230
Middle East, North Africa	20	13	411	391	95.1	244
Latin America, Caribbean	32	14	568	524	92.2	339
Sub-Sahara Africa	44	2	798	81	10.2	414
Totals	184	74	6,808	5,142	75.5	4,178

D1

Nascent Entrepreneur Prevalence:
By Country and Daily Income

Table D1.1

Country	Internet code	$60.01–$407.45/ day	$30.01–$60.00/ day	$15.01–$30.00/ day	$7.501–$15.00/ day	$1.00–$7.50 day	All
Algeria	DZ		10.25	15.83	6.18		10.64
Argentina	AR	9.15	7.00	4.77			6.71
Australia	AU	4.45	3.32				4.15
Austria	AT	2.36					2.36
Belgium	BE	1.63					1.63
Bolivia	BO		17.95		12.15	10.83	12.86
Bosnia and Herzegovina	BA		6.22	4.14	3.89		4.79
Brazil	BR	5.09		4.54	3.26		3.93
Canada	CA	4.92	4.20				4.63
Chile	CL	7.99	7.85	6.71			7.49
China	CH		7.46	4.01		3.31	4.69
Colombia	CO	15.54		10.80		7.30	10.12
Croatia	HR	5.28	3.12	2.37			3.52
Czech Republic	CZ	3.81	1.26				3.23
Denmark	DK	1.74	1.45				1.64
Dominican Republic	DO	10.21		7.47	6.46		8.25
Ecuador	EC	7.87		5.20	2.17		5.42
Egypt	EG		9.57	9.23	5.34		7.06
Finland	FI	2.02					2.02
France	FR	2.32	2.41				2.35

(*Continued*)

Table D1.1   (*Continued*)

Country	Internet code	$60.01–$407.45/ day	$30.01–$60.00/ day	$15.01–$30.00/ day	$7.501–$15.00/ day	$1.00–$7.50 day	All
Germany	DE	2.52	1.74				2.25
Greece	GR	3.42	2.30				3.08
Guatemala	GT		14.37		8.11		10.81
Hong Kong	HK	2.46	1.05				2.07
Hungary	HU	2.71	1.44				1.86
Iceland	IS	4.31	3.39				4.04
India	IN			6.27	5.35	6.40	6.00
Indonesia	ID			4.34	5.72	4.98	5.15
Iran	IR	8.19	5.20	3.99			5.83
Ireland	IE	3.00					3.00
Israel	IL	3.04	2.14				2.73
Italy	IT	1.75	1.98				1.84
Jamaica	JM	8.97		11.68	8.34		9.80
Japan	JP	1.23					1.23
Jordan	JO		5.61		5.57		5.58
Kazakhstan	KZ	4.97	4.88	3.03			3.77
Korea, Republic of	KR	3.71		2.38			3.33
Latvia	LV	5.37	2.74	1.07			3.29
Lebanon	LB	5.96	5.04		2.89		5.00
Macedonia, FYR	MK		8.56	6.85	2.43		6.63
Malaysia	MY	1.95	4.20	4.96			3.53
Mexico	MX	9.14	7.94		4.87		7.09
Morocco	MA			5.35	9.12		7.32
Netherlands	NL	1.41					1.41
New Zealand	NZ	6.43	6.65				6.51
Norway	NO	3.01					3.01
Panama	PA	5.27	5.00		6.54		5.39
Peru	PE	19.78		18.89	16.96		18.29
Philippines	PH		4.56		3.29	2.67	3.57
Poland	PL	4.17	2.10	2.42			2.71
Portugal	PT	3.60	1.69				2.99
Romania	RO	4.26	1.27	1.20			2.33
Russian Federation	RU	1.77	1.29	1.21			1.43
Saudi Arabia	SA	2.42	3.42				2.69
Serbia and Montenegro	RS		3.27	3.61			3.39
Singapore	SG	2.45					2.45
Slovenia	SI	2.54	1.06				2.08
South Africa	ZA	3.57		3.66	3.34		3.54
Spain	ES	2.89	1.85				2.53
Sweden	SE	1.40					1.40
Switzerland	SW	2.75	2.31				2.61
Syria	SY			4.66	3.21	1.18	3.24
Thailand	TH	5.29		4.90	6.76		5.67
Tonga	TO		6.86		8.36		7.80

(*Continued*)

Table D1.1   (*Continued*)

Country	Internet code	$60.01– $407.45/ day	$30.01– $60.00/ day	$15.01– $30.00/ day	$7.501– $15.00/ day	$1.00– $7.50 day	All
Tunisia	TN		2.46	1.00	1.30		1.68
Turkey	TR	3.93	1.34	1.88			1.89
Uganda	UG				11.81	8.13	8.92
United Arab Emirates	AE	4.28	2.18				3.93
United Kingdom	UK	2.41	2.19				2.32
United States	US	6.23	5.78				6.11
Uruguay	UY	9.36	7.04	5.94			7.61
Venezuela	VE	13.19	13.55		14.85		13.81
West Bank/Gaza	PS			2.36	1.89	1.92	2.17
Yemen, Republic of	YE			13.58		25.43	20.68

D2

New Firm Owner Prevalence: By Country and Daily Income

Table D2.1

Country	Internet code	$60.01–$407.45/ day	$30.01–$60.00/ day	$15.01–$30.00/ day	$7.501–$15.00/ day	$1.00–$7.50 day	All
Algeria	DZ		5.94	0.87	2.82		3.34
Argentina	AR	6.41	5.00	3.93			4.96
Australia	AU	5.79	3.51				5.18
Austria	AT	1.48					1.48
Belgium	BE	0.82					0.82
Bolivia	BO		13.06		10.87	11.12	11.42
Bosnia and Herzegovina	BA		1.22	0.80	1.03		1.01
Brazil	BR	9.43		9.42	6.43		7.72
Canada	CA	3.66	1.94				2.96
Chile	CL	4.78	4.02	3.55			4.08
China	CH		11.21	7.79		6.60	8.25
Colombia	CO	8.79		8.71		10.54	9.59
Croatia	HR	2.30	0.92	0.51			1.20
Czech Republic	CZ	1.56	0.48				1.31
Denmark	DK	2.84	1.48				2.35
Dominican Republic	DO	10.38		5.60	5.83		7.44
Ecuador	EC	11.03		8.32	7.03		9.01
Egypt	EG		6.34	4.05	1.60		3.06

(*Continued*)

Table D2.1　(*Continued*)

Country	Internet code	$60.01–$407.45/ day	$30.01–$60.00/ day	$15.01–$30.00/ day	$7.501–$15.00/ day	$1.00–$7.50 day	All
Finland	FI	2.33					2.33
France	FR	0.89	0.68				0.82
Germany	DE	2.36	1.23				1.97
Greece	GR	2.88	1.36				2.41
Guatemala	GT		2.90		2.62		2.74
Hong Kong	HK	1.88	0.32				1.45
Hungary	HU	3.01	1.49				1.99
Iceland	IS	4.33	2.33				3.74
India	IN			4.96	3.92	2.13	3.12
Indonesia	ID			11.05	10.13	7.38	9.49
Iran	IR	4.84	2.89	1.63			3.15
Ireland	IE	3.17					3.17
Israel	IL	2.79	1.18				2.25
Italy	IT	1.52	1.29				1.43
Jamaica	JM	9.07		9.95	5.58		8.22
Japan	JP	1.18					1.18
Jordan	JO		8.28		3.93		5.83
Kazakhstan	KZ	4.89	5.18	3.03			3.84
Korea, Republic of	KR	8.62		4.62			7.48
Latvia	LV	3.65	1.50	0.48			2.04
Lebanon	LB	7.82	8.15		7.44		7.85
Macedonia, FYR	MK		6.19	2.61	2.26		3.64
Malaysia	MY	3.62	2.40	3.70			3.20
Mexico	MX	3.26	2.06		1.16		2.01
Morocco	MA			16.57	1.58		8.71
Netherlands	NL	2.26					2.26
New Zealand	NZ	8.05	5.23				7.07
Norway	NO	3.59					3.59
Panama	PA	3.05	1.57		1.51		2.21
Peru	PE	6.60		8.40	11.03		9.06
Philippines	PH		11.44		12.36	10.50	11.63
Poland	PL	4.51	3.06	1.91			2.96
Portugal	PT	2.89	1.04				2.30
Romania	RO	2.39	0.29	0.23			1.03
Russian Federation	RU	2.87	1.83	0.33			1.71
Saudi Arabia	SA	1.11	0.92				1.06
Serbia and Montenegro	RS		2.87	2.19			2.63
Singapore	SG	2.18					2.18
Slovenia	SI	1.80	0.63				1.44
South Africa	ZA	1.68		1.14	1.79		1.54
Spain	ES	2.40	1.45				2.07
Sweden	SE	2.21					2.21
Switzerland	SW	3.09	2.66				2.96
Syria	SY			5.68	4.54	1.87	4.26

(*Continued*)

Table D2.1 (*Continued*)

Country	Internet code	$60.01–$407.45/ day	$30.01–$60.00/ day	$15.01–$30.00/ day	$7.501–$15.00/ day	$1.00–$7.50 day	All
Thailand	TH	16.93		14.25	10.79		13.63
Tonga	TO		1.31		1.78		1.61
Tunisia	TN		3.13	4.48	2.21		3.59
Turkey	TR	4.21	2.64	1.64			2.53
Uganda	UG				17.56	18.72	18.47
United Arab Emirates	AE	3.43	1.11				3.04
United Kingdom	UK	3.12	2.19				2.74
United States	US	4.12	2.18				3.58
Uruguay	UY	4.85	2.12	1.39			2.94
Venezuela	VE	5.91	7.08		5.44		6.22
West Bank/Gaza	PS			5.89	4.07	3.08	4.91

E

Sources, Measures of Independent Variables for Regression Analysis

	Initial source	Time period (approx)	Notes
Economic Characteristics			
Economic development: GDP per Capita 2009	WEO(1)	2009	
Recent increase in GDP per Capita: 2005–2008	WEO(1)	2005–2008	
Recent population increase: 1999–2009	(2)	1999–2009	
Income inequality	(3)	2000–2008	
Structural Features of the Economy			
Structure of existing economy: Enterprise size	GEM (4)	2000–2009	
Sector emphasis: % of agriculture employment	WB (5)	2000–2007	
Sector emphasis: % of industry employment	WB (5)	2000–2007	
Sector emphasis: % of service employment	WB (5)	2000–2007	

(Continued)

Table E.2   (*Continued*)

	Initial source	Time period (approx)	Notes
Centralized Control, Economic Regulation			
Government employees as per cent of labor force	ILO (6)	2005	
Government expenditures as proportion of GDP	HF (7)	2009	
Business registration complications index	WB (8)	2009	3 item index
Commercial legal contracts cost index	WB (8)	2009	2–3 item indices
Legal recognition of physical property index	IPR (9)	2009	3 item index
Legal recognition of intellectual property index	IPR (9)	2009	3 item index
Perception of corruption	TI (10)	2005	13 sources
Population Capacity for Business Creation			
Entrepreneurial ready citizens	GEM	2000–2009	3 item index
Percent population 25–44 years in age	(2)	2007	
Percent population 15+ years w secondary degree	(11)	2000	
Labor force participation: men	WB (12)	2007	
Labor force participation: women	WB (12)	2007	
Unemployment rate	WB (13)	2000–2008	
National Cultural and Social Norms			
Prevalence of informal investors	GEM	2000–2009	
Cultural support for entrepreneurship	GEM	2000–2009	3 item index
National Values: Traditional versus secular/rational	WVS (14)	1981–2006	Multi-item index
National Values: Survival versus self-expressive	WVS (14)	1981–2006	Multi-item index

Sources: (1) World Economic Outlook, October 2009. (2) US Census International Data Base. (3) Solt (2009). (4) GEM survey prevalence of established firms, with profits for over 42 months. (5) World Bank data series. (6) International Labor Organization, LABORSTA, Public Sector Employment. (7) World Bank Labor Force Total for 2009. (8) From data set provided to accompany La Porta et al. (2008). (7) Heritage Foundation, Index of Economic Freedom, 2005 data sets "www.heritage.org/index/2005." (8) World Bank Doing Business 2010 report, ratio index created from average of values on number of procedures, time to completion, and cost to register. (9) International Property Rights Index: 2010 Report, Strokova (2010). (10) Transparency International, "www.transparency.org," for 2005. (11) Barro and Lee (2000) for 1980. (12) World Bank Genderstat data base for 2007 in April 2010. (13) World Bank. (14) Inglehart and Welzel (2005) and data set provided on the project Web site.

F

High, Medium, and Low Income Countries by Daily Income

Table F.1

	High income	Medium income	Low income
GDP per capita: maximum	US$ 57,534 (PPP)	US$ 35,000 (PPP)	US$ 16,000 (PPP)
GDP per capita: Minimum	US$ 35,000 (PPP)	US$ 16,000 (PPP)	US$ 1,041 (PPP)
Average value	US$ 41,697 (PPP)	US$ 25,688 (PPP)	US$ 8,923 (PPP)
All countries	AU, AT, BE, CA, DK, FI, FR, DE, HK, IS, IE, JP, NL, NO, SG, SE, SW, AE, UK, US	HR, CZ, GR, HU, IL, IT, KR, LV, NZ, PL, PT, RU, SA, SI, ES	DZ, AR, BO, BA, BR, CL, CH, CO, DO, EG, EC, GT, IN, ID, IR, JM, JO, KZ, LB, MK, MY, MX, MA, PA, PE, PH, RO, RS, ZA, SY, TH, TN, TO, TR, UG, UY, VE, PS
Daily income: $60–$407	AU, AT, BE, CA, DK, FI, FR, DE, HK, IS, IE, JP, NL, NO, SG, SE, SW, AE, UK, US	HR, CZ, GR, HU, IL, IT, KR, LV, NZ, PL, PT, RU, SA, SI, ES	AR, BR, CL, CO, DO, EC, IR, JM, KZ, LB, MY, MX, PA, PE, RO, ZA, TH, TR, UY, VE

(Continued)

Table F.2   (*Continued*)

	High income	Medium income	Low income
Daily income: $30–$60	AU, CA, DK, FR, DE, HK, IS, SW, AE, UK, US	HR, CZ, GR, HU, IL, IT, LV, NZ, PL, PT, RU, SA, SI, ES	DZ, AR, BO, BA, CL, CH, EG, GT, IR, JM, JO, KZ, LB, MK, MY, MX, PA, PH, RO, RS, TO, TN, TR, UY
Daily income: $15–$30		HR, KR, LV, PL, RU	DZ, AR, BA, BR, CL, CH, CO, DO, EG, EC, IN, ID, IR, JM, KZ, MK, MY, MA, PE, RO, RS, ZA, SY, TH, TR, TN, UY, PS
Daily income: $1–$15.00			DZ, BO, BA, BR, CH, CO, DO, EG, EC, GT, IN, ID, JM, JO, LB, MK, MX, MA, PA, PE, PH, ZA, SY, TH, TO, TN, UG, VE, PS

Source: Entries are the two-character internet code assigned to each country, available in the second column of Appendix D1. Countries are entered alphabetically by their proper name, not by internet code.

G

Coding of Individual Characteristics

Table G.1

Personal attribute	Coded as 0	Coded as 1
Gender	Women	Men
Age: 18–24 years old	Does not apply	Applies
Age: 25–34 years old	Does not apply	Applies
Age: 35–44 years old	Does not apply	Applies
Age: 45–54 years old	Does not apply	Applies
Age: 55–64 years old	Does not apply	Applies
Education: not completed high school	Does not apply	Applies
Education: high school degree	Does not apply	Applies
Education: more than high school, college degree	Does not apply	Applies
Education: any graduate experience	Does not apply	Applies
Labor force activity: working full or part time	Does not apply	Applies
Labor force activity: not working	Does not apply	Applies
Labor force activity: not in the labor force	Does not apply	Applies
Daily income: $1–7.50/day	Does not apply	Applies
Daily income: $7.50–15/day	Does not apply	Applies
Daily income: $15–30/day	Does not apply	Applies
Daily income: $30–60/day	Does not apply	Applies
Daily income: $60–500/day	Does not apply	Applies
Household income: lowest third in country	Does not apply	Applies
Household income: lowest third in country	Does not apply	Applies
Household income: lowest third in country	Does not apply	Applies
Perception of business opportunities	No	Yes
Confidence in personal capacity to start a firm	No	Yes
Know other entrepreneurs	No	Yes
Fear of failure would discourage starting a business	No	Yes

H

Development of Multi-Level Models

Model development with MLM7 involves several steps.[1]

(1) Creating a data set with no missing values for any cases.

(2) Individual case and country weights re-centered such that they both average one.

(3) The nature of the outcome variable is specified, dichotomous or nominal variables in this case. A Bernoulli distribution is assumed to reflect the outcome.

(4) An initial model is developed with no predictors, such that only the error term is included to specific the variance associated with the prediction of the outcome for the country level. This is an estimate of the total variance to be explained, or accounted for, by the development of the linear additive model.

(5) The reliability of the estimate (the ratio of the outcome variance to the total variance (outcome and error) is also

---

[1] Based on Raudenbush and Bryk (2002), Raudenbush et al. (2011), and UCLA Academic Technology Services (2012).

produced.[2] Reliabilities close to 1.00 are indicators of a smaller error of measurement.

(6) A model is then specified by identifying the individual attributes and national attributes expected to have a significant impact on the outcome.

(7) The output analysis specifies both the coefficients associated with each independent variable and the statistical significance associated with individual and national predictors.

(8) Those that have a less than statistically significant impact on the linear additive model are then removed and a new model is estimated.

(9) For national (level 2) characteristics, a procedure included in HLM7 allows estimating the statistical significance of the impact omitted variables if they had been incorporated into the predictive model. This is helpful in ensuring that all variables with a statistically significant impact have been incorporate in the assessment.

(10) A file with the residuals (errors of prediction for each case) is also produced, which can be examined to determine if they are normally distributed; this is an indication that the major assumptions associated with model development have been met.

(11) Comparison of the variance associated with the final predictions with that associated with Step 4 provides an estimate of the variance across countries accounted for by the final model.

The procedure involves some trial and error, as often removing one predictor may affect the impact of other predictors. The impact of each model on the explained variance in the outcome, the reliability, and the distribution of the residuals is helpful in selecting an optimal final model.

Step 1 involved excluding all cases with missing values. Once all the independent and dependent variables were identified, the entire sample

---

[2] Raudenbush and Bryk, (2002, p. 46).

of 1.21 million cases was reviewed to determine the extent of missing values. There was, of course, no issue with the variables representing national characteristics; this data was available for all countries. However, variables related to the individual factors were missing for a substantial number of cases, for the reasons discussed previously. The final data set includes 72 countries and 583,127 cases. Individual case weights were re-centered such that the average value within each country was one. As in the prior assessments, the national weights that reflected the proportion of the total population of those 18–64 represented by each country were re-centered such that the average value was one.

11

Multi-Level Models: Nascent Entrepreneurs by Daily Income

Table I1.1

Daily per capita income	All	$60–$407/ day	$30–$60/ day	$15–$30/ day	$1–$15/ day
Number of countries	72	55	49	32	28
Individual respondents	583,127	341,388	155,109	44,591	42,039
Percent cross national variance explained	76.8%	82.8%	68.0%	70.6%	81.0%
Reliability	0.85	0.83	0.81	0.69	0.40
Nascent/100 adults: national (weighted average)	4.78	4.25	4.62	5.60	7.25
Constant	−3.32	−3.41	−3.32	−3.12	−3.07
Individual Characteristics					
Gender: (men = 1; women = 0)	0.18	0.19		0.07	0.25
Age: 18–24 years old	*Base	Base	Base	Base	Base
Age: 25–34 years old	−0.18			−0.47	
Age: 35–44 years old	−0.38	−0.16		−0.66	−0.29
Age: 45–54 years old	−0.56	−0.34	−0.46	−0.54	−0.53
Age: 55–64 years old	−0.78	−0.72	−0.56	−0.66	−0.87
Education: no HS degree	Base	Base	Base	Base	Base
Education: HS degree	0.32	0.10	0.19	0.34	0.33
Education: post HS, college degree	0.39	0.16	0.50	0.47	
Education: graduate experience	0.34	0.14		0.49	

(*Continued*)

Table I1.2   (*Continued*)

Daily per capita income	All	$60–$407/ day	$30–$60/ day	$15–$30/ day	$1–$15/ day
Working full, part time	0.45		0.49	0.42	
Not currently working	0.52		0.48	0.30	
Not in labor force	Base	Base	Base	Base	Base
Household Inc: lower third for country		0.42		−0.34	−0.30
Household Inc: middle third for country		0.25	0.24		−0.59
Household Inc: upper third for country		Base	Base	Base	Base
Perceive opportunities	0.72	0.82	0.71	0.65	0.70
Confidence in start-up skills	1.06	1.52	0.97	0.89	0.85
Know an entrepreneur	0.59	0.60	0.60	0.70	0.55
Fear of failure effect		−0.22			
Economic Characteristics					
GDP per capita below US$ 16,000/yr	0.79	0.60	1.07		
GDP per capita: US$ 16,000 and US$ 35,000/yr	Base	Base	Base	Base	N/A
GDP per capita above US$ 35,000/yr	0.25		0.80	N/A	N/A
Percent change GDP per capita					
Structural Features of the Economy					
Prevalence of nascent firms (#/100 persons)	N/A	N/A	N/A	N/A	N/A
Prevalence of new firms (#/100 persons)	0.04				
Prevalence of established firms (#/100) persons					
Percent agricultural workers: 2009	−0.02	−0.02			
Centralized Control of Economic Activity					
Population Capacity for Business Creation					
National index: readiness for entrepreneurship	N/A	N/A	N/A	N/A	N/A
Percent women 15–64 yrs labor force: 2007					
National Cultural and Social Support					
Prevalence informal investors: #/100 Persons	0.12	0.18	0.12	0.10	0.08
National index: support for entrepreneurship					
Traditional (+1) vs. secular/rational (−1) values	0.18	0.26		0.30	0.26

*Base: Not included in regression models to provide a base for comparison.
N/A: Not applicable, no cases in this cell for this analysis.

12

Multi-Level Models: New Firm Owners by Daily Income

Table 12.1

Daily per capita income	All	$60–$407/ day	$30–$60/ day	$15–$30/ day	$1–$15/ day
Number of countries	72	55	49	32	28
Individual respondents	583,127	341,388	155,109	44,591	42,039
Percent cross national variance explained	92.4%	77.9%	96.7%	97.1%	97.8%
Reliability	0.79	0.87	0.50	0.34	0.21
New firms/100 adults: national (weighted average)	4.19	3.62	3.36	5.60	6.60
Constant	−3.31	−3.40	−3.57	−3.34	−2.97
Individual Characteristics					
Gender: (men = 1; women = 0)		0.18		−0.14	
Age: 18–24 years old	*Base	Base	Base	Base	Base
Age: 25–34 years old	0.35	0.30		0.40	0.45
Age: 35–44 years old					
Age: 45–54 years old					
Age: 55–64 years old	−0.29	−0.29	−0.47	−0.87	
Education: no HS degree	Base	Base	Base	Base	Base
Education: HS degree			−0.27	−0.28	
Education: post HS, college degree			−0.64	−0.57	
Education: graduate experience	−0.17		−0.41	−0.55	

(*Continued*)

Table I2.2   (*Continued*)

Daily per capita income	All	$60–$407/ day	$30–$60/ day	$15–$30/ day	$1–$15/ day
Working full, part time	N/A	N/A	N/A	N/A	N/A
Not currently working	N/A	N/A	N/A	N/A	N/A
Not in labor force	N/A	N/A	N/A	N/A	N/A
Household Inc: lower third for country	−0.32				
Household Inc: middle third for country	−0.17				0.81
Household Inc: upper third for country	Base	Base	Base	Base	Base
Perceive opportunities	0.25	0.38	0.36	0.20	
Confidence in start-up skills	1.06	1.59	1.05	0.83	1.00
Know an entrepreneur	0.41	0.63	0.51	0.32	0.24
Fear of failure effect	−0.33	−0.48	−0.41		−0.26
Economic Characteristics					
GDP per capita below US$ 16,000/yr					
GDP per capita: US$ 16,000 and US$ 35,000/yr	Base	Base	Base	Base	N/A
GDP per capita above US$ 35,000/yr				N/A	N/A
Percent change GDP per capita		0.06	0.07		
Structural Features of the Economy					
Prevalence of nascent firms (#/100 persons)	0.07		0.08		
Prevalence of new firms (#/100 persons)	N/A	N/A	N/A	N/A	N/A
Prevalence of established firms (#/100) persons	0.10	0.12	0.13	0.12	0.06
Percent agricultural workers: 2009					
Centralized Control of Economic Activity					
Ease of business registration index				0.32	
Population Capacity for Business Creation					
National Index: readiness for entrepreneurship	N/A	N/A	N/A	N/A	N/A
Percent women 15–64 yrs labor force: 2007	0.01	0.01			0.03
National Cultural and Social Support					
Prevalence informal investors: #/100 Persons	−0.07			−0.07	
National index: support for entrepreneurship	0.32			0.51	
Traditional (+1) vs. secular/rational (−1) values		0.30			0.24

*Base: Not included in regression models to provide a base for comparison.
N/A: Not applicable, no cases in this cell for this analysis.

J1

Multi-Level Models: Perceive Opportunity by Daily Income

Table J1.1

Daily per capita income	All	$60–$407/ day	$30–$60/ day	$15–$30/ day	$1–$15/ day
Number of countries	72	55	49	32	28
Individual respondents	583,127	341,388	155,109	44,591	42,039
Percent cross national variance explained	79.2%	79.7%	81.6%	76.0%	76.8%
Reliability	0.96	0.96	0.86	0.92	0.70
Proportion reporting "yes"	32%	32%	28%	35%	42%
Constant	−0.77	−0.74	0.00	−0.77	−0.44
Individual Characteristics					
Gender: (men = 1; women = 0)	0.26	0.35	0.53	0.19	−0.29
Age: 18–24 years old	*Base	Base	Base	Base	Base
Age: 25–34 years old	−0.08		0.34	−0.31	
Age: 35–44 years old	−0.22	−0.07	0.34	−0.31	
Age: 45–54 years old	−0.29	−0.16	0.34	−0.34	−0.28
Age: 55–64 years old	−0.40	−0.23	0.16	−0.71	−0.38
Education: no HS degree	Base	Base	Base	Base	Base
Education: HS degree			0.10		
Education: post HS, college degree			0.22	0.16	0.34
Education: graduate experience	0.22	0.17	0.36		

(Continued)

137

Table J1.2   (*Continued*)

Daily per capita income	All	$60–$407/ day	$30–$60/ day	$15–$30/ day	$1–$15/ day
Working full, part time	0.34	0.08	0.64	0.29	0.66
Not currently working			0.24		
Not in labor force	Base	Base	Base	Base	Base
Household Inc: lower third for country	−0.22	−0.36	−0.28		
Household Inc: middle third for country	−0.14	−0.19			
Household Inc: upper third for country	Base	Base	Base	Base	Base
Economic Characteristics					
GDP Per capita below US$ 16,000/yr	0.36		0.95		
GDP Per capita: US$ 16,000 and US$ 35,000/yr	Base	Base	Base	Base	N/A
GDP Per capita above US$ 35,000/yr		−0.52		N/A	N/A
Percent change GDP per capita: 2003–2008	0.06	0.07		0.15	
Population increase: 1999–2009	0.35	0.24	0.35	0.67	0.59
Structural Features of the Economy					
Prevalence of nascent firms (#/100 persons)					
Prevalence of new firms (#/100 persons)					
Prevalence of established firms (#/100) persons					
Percent agricultural workers: 2009					
Centralized Control of Economic Activity					
Ease of business registration index					
Population Capacity for Business Creation					
National Index: readiness for entrepreneurship	N/A	N/A	N/A	N/A	N/A
Percent women 15–64 yrs labor force: 2007					
National Cultural and Social Support					
Prevalence informal investors: #/100 persons					
National index: support for entrepreneurship					
Traditional (+1) vs. secular/rational (−1) values	0.17	0.22		0.54	
Survival (+1) vs. self-expressive (−1) values	−0.35	−0.56	−0.27		

J2

Multi-Level Models: Confidence in Start-Up Skills by Daily Income

Table J2.1

Daily per capita income	All	$60–$407/ day	$30–$60/ day	$15–$30/ day	$1–$15/ day
Number of countries	72	55	49	32	28
Individual respondents	583,127	341,388	155,109	44,591	42,039
Percent cross national variance explained	85.2%	81.5%	78.6%	87.2%	95.3%
Reliability	0.95	0.96	0.89	0.87	0.54
Proportion reporting "yes"	50%	51%	45%	52%	58%
Constant	−0.06	0.11	0.00	−0.13	0.30
Individual Characteristics					
Gender: (men = 1; women = 0)	0.48	0.62	0.53	0.41	0.30
Age: 18–24 years old	*Base	Base	Base	Base	Base
Age: 25–34 years old	0.17	0.42	0.34		
Age: 35–44 years old	0.16	0.52	0.34		
Age: 45–54 years old		0.46	0.34	−0.31	
Age: 55–64 years old		0.50	0.16	−0.29	−0.34
Education: no HS degree	Base	Base	Base	Base	Base
Education: HS degree	0.21	0.11	0.10	0.16	0.38
Education: post HS, college degree	0.29	0.25	0.22		0.41
Education: graduate experience	0.37	0.33	0.36		0.49

(*Continued*)

Table J2.2 (*Continued*)

Daily per capita income	All	$60–$407/ day	$30–$60/ day	$15–$30/ day	$1–$15/ day
Working full, part time	0.56	0.37	0.64	0.91	0.75
Not currently working		0.06	0.24	0.20	
Not in labor force	Base	Base	Base	Base	Base
Household Inc: lower third for country	−0.44	−0.42	−0.28		
Household Inc: middle third for country	−0.25	−0.25			0.28
Household Inc: upper third for country	Base	Base	Base	Base	Base
Economic Characteristics					
GDP per capita below US$ 16,000/yr	0.36		0.95		
GDP per capita: US$ 16,000 and US$ 35,000/yr	Base	Base	Base	Base	N/A
GDP per capita above US$ 35,000/yr		−0.55		N/A	N/A
Percent change GDP per capita: 2003–2008	0.06	0.06		0.09	
Population increase: 1999–2009	0.35		0.35		0.56
Structural Features of the Economy					
Prevalence of nascent firms (#/100 persons)					
Prevalence of new firms (#/100 persons)					
Prevalence of established firms (#/100) persons	0.04				0.02
Percent agricultural workers: 2009					
Centralized Control of Economic Activity					
Percent of all workers in government jobs	0.02				
Population Capacity for Business Creation					
National index: readiness for entrepreneurship	N/A	N/A	N/A	N/A	N/A
Percent men 15–64 yrs labor force: 2007				0.08	
Percent women 15–64 yrs labor force: 2007				−0.02	
National Cultural and Social Support					
Prevalence informal investors: #/100 persons					
National index: support for entrepreneurship					
Traditional (+1) vs. secular/rational (−1) values	0.33	0.46		0.66	0.28
Survival (+1) vs. self-expressive (−1) values	−0.40	−0.63	−0.27		

J3

Multi-Level Models: Know Another Entrepreneur by Daily Income

Table J3.1

Daily per capita income	All	$60–$407/ day	$30–$60/ day	$15–$30/ day	$1–$15/ day
Number of countries	72	55	49	32	28
Individual respondents	583,127	341,388	155,109	44,591	42,039
Percent cross national variance explained	63.2%	48.4%	86.9%	73.4%	82.2%
Reliability	0.96	0.96	0.90	0.89	0.50
Proportion reporting "yes"	40%	42%	35%	42%	44%
Constant	−0.29	−0.16	−0.20	−0.30	−0.27
Individual Characteristics					
Gender: (men = 1; women = 0)	0.29	0.39	0.28	0.27	0.15
Age: 18–24 years old	*Base	Base	Base	Base	Base
Age: 25–34 years old					0.25
Age: 35–44 years old	−0.18	−0.16	−0.22	−0.26	
Age: 45–54 years old	−0.43	−0.40	−0.48	−0.64	
Age: 55–64 years old	−0.52	−0.54	−0.72	−0.64	
Education: no HS degree	Base	Base	Base	Base	Base
Education: HS degree	0.22		0.15		0.43
Education: post HS, college degree	0.37	0.16	0.23	0.28	0.66
Education: graduate experience	0.51	0.31	0.49		0.92
Working full, part time	0.35	0.26	0.39	0.48	0.42
Not currently working					

(*Continued*)

Table J3.2   (*Continued*)

Daily per capita income	All	$60–$407/ day	$30–$60/ day	$15–$30/ day	$1–$15/ day
Not in labor force	Base	Base	Base	Base	Base
Household Inc: lower third for country	−0.46	−0.45	−0.40		
Household Inc: middle third for country	−0.23	−0.24	−0.22		
Household Inc: upper third for country	Base	Base	Base	Base	Base
Economic Characteristics					
GDP per capita below US$ 16,000/yr			1.11		
GDP per capita: US$ 16,000 and US$ 35,000/yr	Base	Base	Base	Base	N/A
GDP per capita above US$ 35,000/yr				N/A	N/A
Percent change GDP per capita: 2003–2008	0.06			0.11	
Population increase: 1999–2009	0.13		0.24	0.51	0.15
Structural Features of the Economy					
Prevalence of nascent firms (#/100 persons)					0.04
Prevalence of new firms (#/100 persons)	0.04				
Prevalence of established firms (#/100) persons				0.04	
Percent agricultural workers: 2009					
Centralized Control of Economic Activity					
Percent of all workers in government jobs					
Legal protection for intellectual property rights		−0.19			
Population Capacity for Business Creation					
National Index: readiness for entrepreneurship	N/A	N/A	N/A	N/A	N/A
Percent men 15–64 yrs labor force: 2007					
Percent women 15–64 yrs labor force: 2007					
National Cultural and Social Support					
Prevalence informal investors: #/100 persons		0.11			
National Index: support for entrepreneurship					
Traditional (+1) vs. secular/rational (−1) values			−0.38		
Survival (+1) vs. self-expressive (−1) values					0.59

References

Barro, R. J. and J.-W. Lee (2000), *International Data on Educational Attainment: Updates and Implications*. Cambridge, MA: Harvard University, Center for international Development. Working Paper 42.

Bornstein, D. (2011), 'Grameen Bank and the Public Good'. *New York Times Opinionator*, 24 March.

Bosma, N. and J. Levie (2010), 'Global Entrepreneurship Monitor: 2009 Executive Report'. Global Entrepreneurship Research Association.

Coase, R. H. (1937), 'The nature of the firm'. *Economica* **4**(16), 386–405.

Collier, P. (2007), *The Bottom Billion: Why the Poorest Countries are Failing and What Can Be Done About It.* New York: Oxford University Press.

de Paula, A. and J. A. Scheinkman (2007), 'The informal sector'. Second Version. Penn Institute for Economic Research Working Paper 07-035. Philadelphia, PA. University of Pennsylvania.

de Soto, H. (2011), 'The free market secret of the Arab revolutions'. *Financial Times* **8**(November).

Goldstone, J. A. (2010), 'The new population bomb: Four megatrends that will change the World'. *Foreign Affairs* **89**(1), 31.

Hecker, D. E. (2005), 'High-tech employment: A NAICS-based update'. *Monthly Labor Review* (July), 57–72.

Hodgson, G. M. (1998), 'The Approach of Institutional Economics'. *Journal of Economic Literature* **36**(1), 166–192.

Hofmann, D. A. (1997), 'An overview of the logic and rationale of hierarchical linear models'. *Journal of Management* **23**(6), 723–744.

Hofmann, D. A. and M. B. Gavin (1998), 'Centering decisions in hierarchical linear models: Implications for research in organizations'. *Journal of Management* **24**(5), 623–641.

Inglehart, R. (1990), *Cultural Shift in Advanced Industrial Society.* Princeton, NJ: Princeton University Press.

Inglehart, R. and C. Welzel (2005), *Modernization, Cultural Change and Democracy.* New York: Cambridge University Press.

Inglehart, R. and C. Welzel (2010), 'Changing mass priorities: The link between modernization and democracy'. *Perspectives on Politics* **8**(2), 554.

International Labour Organization (ILO) (2010), *World of Work Report 2010: From one Crisis to the Next?* Geneva: International Institute for Labour Studies.

International Labour Organization (ILO) (2011), *World of Work Report 2011: Making Markets Work for Jobs.* Geneva: International Institute for Labour Studies.

Kreft, I. and J. de Leeuw (1998), *Introducing Multilevel Modeling.* Thousand Oaks, CA: Sage.

La Porta, R., F. Lopez-de-Silanes, and A. Shleifer (2008), 'The economic consequences of legal origins'. *Journal of Economic Literature* **46**(2), 285–332.

Milanovic, B. (1989), *Liberalization and Entrepreneurship: Dynamics of Reform in Socialism and Capitalism.* Armonk, NY: M. E. Sharpe.

Milanovic, B. (1998), *Income, Inequality, and Poverty during the Transition from Planned to Market Economy.* Washington, DC: The World Bank.

Milanovic, B. (2005), *Worlds Apart: Measuring International and Global Inequality.* Princeton, NJ: Princeton University Press.

Milanovic, B. (2011), *The Haves and the Have-Nots.* New York City: Basic books.

North, D. C. (1990), *Institutions, Institutional Change, and Economic Performance*. New York: Cambridge University Press.

North, D. C. (1993), 'Economic performance through time'. In: L. Alston, T. Eggertsson, and D. C. North (eds.): *Empirical Studies in Institutional Change, Nobel Prize in Economic Science Lecture (1996)*. Cambridge, UK: Cambridge University Press, pp. 342–355.

Pinkovskiy, M. and X. Sala-i-Martin (2009), 'Parametric estimations of the world distribution of income'. Cambridge, MA: National Bureau of Economic Research Working Paper 15433.

Prahalad, C. K. (2010), *The Fortune at the Bottom of the Pyramid: Eradicating Poverty Through Profits*. Upper Saddle River, NJ: Wharton School Publishing, fifth edition.

Raudenbush, S., A. Bryk, Y. F. Cheong, R. Congdon, and M. du Toit (2011), *HLM7: Hierarchical Linear and Nonlinear Modeling*. Lincolnwood, IL: Scientific Software International, Inc.

Raudenbush, S. W. and A. S. Bryk (2002), *Hierarchical Linear Models: Applications and Data Analysis Methods*. Thousand Oaks, CA: Sage, second edition.

Reynolds, P. D. (2011), 'New firm creation: A global assessment of national, contextual, and individual factors'. *Foundations and Trends in Entrepreneurship* **6**(5–6), 315–496.

Reynolds, P. D., N. Bosma, E. Autio, S. Hunt, N. De Bono, and I. Servais et al (2005), 'Global entrepreneurship monitor; Data collection design and implementation, 1998–2003'. *Small Business Economics* **24**, 205–231.

Reynolds, P. D., N. M. Carter, W. B. Gartner, and P. G. Greene (2004), 'The prevalence of nascent entrepreneurs in the United States: Evidence from the panel study of entrepreneurial dynamics'. *Small Business Economics* **43**(4), 263–284.

Reynolds, P. D. and R. T. Curtin (eds.) (2010), *New Firm Creation: An International Overview*. New York: Springer.

Reynolds, P. D. and R. T. Curtin (2011), 'Panel study of entrepreneurial dynamics (PSED I, II): A harmonized data set of transitions and outcomes'. http://psed.isr.umich.edu.

Reynolds, P. D. and B. Miller (1992), 'New firm gestation: Conception, birth, and implications for research'. *Journal of Business Venturing* **7**(5), 405–417.

Rosen, L. (2010), 'Understanding corruption'. *The American Interest* (March-April).

Schumpeter, J. A. (1934), *The Theory of Economic Development*. Cambridge, MA: Harvard University Press.

Shah, A. (2010), 'Global issues'. http://www.global issues.org, updated September 20.

Solt, F. (2009), 'Standardizing the world income inequality database'. *Social Science Quarterly* **90**(2), 231–242.

Strokova, V. (2010), *International Property Rights Index: 2010 Report*. Washington, DC: American for Tax Reform Foundation/Property Rights Alliance.

Strom, S. (2011), 'Couple donate $150 million to fight poverty in developing nations'. *New York Times* **4**(November).

UCLA Academic Technology Services (2012), *Statistical Computing Seminar: Introduction to Multilevel Modeling Using HLM*. Santa Monica, CA: University of California at Los Angeles. http://www.ats.ucla.edu/stat/hlm/eminars/hlm_mlm/608/mlm_hlm_seminar_v608.html' (accessed 1 March 2012).

United Nations University (2011), *World Income Inequality Database: User Guide and Data Sources*. New York City: United Nations University-World Institute for Development Economics Research (accessed 2 January 2012).

Weidemann Associates (2011), 'The entrepreneurship toolkit'. *Prepared for the US Department of State, USAID, Business Growth Initiative*. Contract EEM-C-00-06-00022-00.

Wennekers, S., A. van Stel, R. Thurik, and P. Reynolds (2005), 'Nascent entrepreneurship and the level of economic development'. *Small Business Economics* **24**(3), 293–309.

World Bank (2009), *Doing Business 2010*. New York: Palgrave MacMillan.

Lightning Source UK Ltd.
Milton Keynes UK
UKOW04f0222150414

229989UK00001B/94/P